I0434552

Shinvescarine Equasion
Bacterium Living
Consequence

Holsinger Cosmology of Shinvescarine

Shinvescarine Equasion Bacterium Living Consequence

✦

Humanistic Sexologist Theoreum

Bacterium Living Consequence Idea of Germ Desire

Written By Damon Ray Hollingsworth PH.D. Doctor of Divinity

Writers Club Press

San Jose New York Lincoln Shanghai

Shinvescarine Equasion Bacterium Living Consequence
Humanistic Sexologist Theoreum

Writers Club Press
an imprint of iUniverse, Inc.

For information address:
iUniverse, Inc.
5220 S. 16th St., Suite 200
Lincoln, NE 68512
www.iuniverse.com

ISBN: 0-595-23432-1

Printed in the United States of America

BABYLON

You ask me, how I live
You lousy Minx, you send out all the signals
I ought to have you spade, ingenious costume
First'fund goody=goody:

SOLFEGIO

MIMI
May, Me, My, Mow, Moo
At last the Sun sets and rises with you
MIMI Ethiopia is class task
Catch back relax facts on the fast track
MIMI: mine is count, what I got
MIMI: mine is count, what I am
MIMI: is mind, matter physical laughter
MIMI is MIMIC Systemic
Heirloom, breath sculpturing jewels
Humanlife as finishing brings, the exotic vibrant
porcelain

Contents

Humanistic Sexologist Theoreum [1]

Humanistic Sexologist Theoreum [2]

Humanistic Sexologist Theoreum [3]

Afterword

The Faith factor to understand the fundamental differences, between true thinking and the living cycle, sculpture according to energy itself performing thoughts, stature by revolving with time and living, learning knowledge existing.

Preface Acknowledgement

My philosophy and this Book is that to examine issues current, feelings spoken cues that trigger responential language, our Human sexuality economics translate express beauty, universe of man, science approbation and patronage of vastness human service employs Good health, principality and majesty evolving honour, revolving growth Genuine importance, as journeys beyond stars midst.

Reciprocation "planisphere esoteric hemisphere"

Perhaps we will bear any burden, support any friend to assure and meet Survival libertarian functions the instincts drives responsibility of subject judgement, by which means continuation of peace and prosperity, act.

"[The Mind is the opportunity to show through knowledge intelligence.]" Because one of Flesh Hardwater' Smoothtalk; the art proven techniques. Can Babies join reality, yet though they have Wives? Yes, they can.

The acquisitions to draw views, draw between compromise and the accuracy analysis performing to expend performing the analysis He and/of She "eh" thinks they need paradox life aesthetics predilective exhuberance of classicism linguistics face exciting style expressive aesthetics. The analysis thereby acquires consequences theme of substances to exploited term realism, leading gender receipt, global livingstone on reacting bone, awareness structuring, here's patience of bath, mind pathology activating praise. The Faith factor to understand the Fundamental differences between true thinking and the living cycle of Course, Beside art. Painting.

Beside art, Painting

Damon Ray Hollingsworth PH.D. Business Principles and Management

Glossary

A
I and OF

Abdominal
Between the thorax and the pelvis, belly

Absorption
To take in by molecular and/of chemical action

Academic
Conforming to set rules

Acknowledgement
Truism of the existence

Acquiesce
Submit, comply without protest

Adrenaline
Energizer

Aegis
Sponsorship, support, protection

Aeroplanea
Bacterium move aerobe sonic supersonic aesthete ethereal the Upper atmosphere ooze and coil afferent pledging toward change, a nerve of star

Aesthetic
Sensitivity of feeling, a idea

Aestheticism
The acceptance of aesthetic supreme importance

Aesthetics
Particular philosophy of beauty

Allegiance
Pledge of proceeding some act toward Shinvescarine as being Holsinger and the HOLY GHOST

Anomaly
Now and then at another time arrangement star, strange

Apathy
Representing the assumed movement, rather than riding with Probability and Correspondence

APNEA
To allow alertness specified feeling with breathing during gesture of sexualism, human foreplay-intravaginal stimulating

Apropos
Being opportunely, timely

Assiduity
Devoted diligence, attentive application

Assiduous
The exchange and goodwill diligently at task works, Jobing.

Autistic
Characterized self absorption

BABB
Speak, Talk

Babylon
Prattle of which deeply affectionate

Back
Torso upper backside

Backruptcy
Method, means setting place of doctrine improving developing method

Bacteriology
Dealing with bacteria

Bacterium
Nitrogen fixation, fermentation and smells

Barracuda
Fish genus Sphyraena, of warm seas, and large and striking Sharp teeth

Bass
Numerous serranidae and centrarchidae spiny finned, fresh Marine water fish

Biochronic
Life and long lasting

Biologic
Living processes matter characteristics

Biosynthesis
Forming compounds by acting chemicals

BOOK OF LIFE
The anterior part of central nervous system, jelly enclosed in the cranium of vertebrates, consisting of a mass of nerve tissue organized for the perception of sensory impulses, the regulation of motor impulses,

and the production of memory, learning, conscience and conscious-ness, meanings. The ulterior Brain:

Camel
Camelus: genus large effective and Humped
Bactrian Camelism, ranging Dromedary aperture of Camelism Beast

Camel'=Hair
camel's hair, genus ruminants camelist' camelus' camelism,
camel'=hair follicle and camelus cloth hair'follicle and White, Pink, Red, Brown, Black Hirsute as shaggy keratinous filaments hairy and numerous cylindrical living growth filaments keratinous coat covering growth ruminants camelism

Camelism
camelus bactrianus: Two'humps carrying backside itself
camelus dromedarius: 6 feet 1.8 meters high at shoulders
length 9 ½ feet 2.9 meters singular hump, singular hump singularity

Camelist
The understood doctrine understanding Gib'Ral'-Tar, realm Manstar:
Beastiality of Styme Bow World 7th Star
Vis' a' Vis Damon Ray Hollingsworth PH.D.
Held chemistry of Juice' Pit' Turn:

Camelus
Camel'=like, underlying growth Gib'Ral'-Tar, Realm
camel like, underlying growth Styme Bow World, Damon Ray Holl-ingsworth, Doctor of Philosophy of Religion, Luke: chapter 18 verse 25:
Camelus Dromedarius, The American state outline of Canada and South America as umbilical link Heart. Doctor of Biblical Counseling Damon Ray Hollingsworth PH.D. Mark: chapter 10 verse 25.

Canal
Tublar watercourse of channel passage

Cardiovascular
Systemic hart and blood vessels channeling

Causative
Produce acting, cause of producing

Cavity
Womb, vagina

Cerebrovascular
Conscious processes voluntary with movement

Cirrus
Thin white altitude of filaments veil cloud

Civilization
Culture and state of specific time

Clandestine
Acting purpose of secrecy

Climactic
Culminating held by which change occur characterized over a series of movement

Clitoral
The erectile organic skinflesh top of vulva area incis.on

Coil
Disturbance a noisey ado

Consequence
Self-important matter progressing

Constriction
Stop the course of development

Contraindication
To undo a procedure

Convection
The act of conveying movement transmitting liquid

Creative
Imaginative originality with thought to arrange existence as being collective

Crico'=pharyngeus
Nasal portion, the articulated membranes and muscles that connects the nasal passages with larynx

Cumulus
Pile of forms, mounds, puffs flat bases cloud heaps

Datum
Surface used measuring reference

Desire
Suitable attractive arousing hunger as it stood passion

Desperado
The state of being the extreme undertaken need

DNA
Carries genes strands molecule arranged segments

Doctrinaire
Characteristic dogmatic preacher regarding theoristic view.

Ecosystem
Community organisms system formed by interacting with the environment

Ejaculatory
The act discharging by ejecting sperm, reproductive organs

Emotive
Activating pertinent feelings.

Empirical
Experience of senses

Epic
Resembling majestic form

Epidermis
A thin layer of cells forming skin.

Epitome
Features of whole embodiment

Equasion
State of being symbolic representation starting reacting materials

Equilibrium
Resembling sense existing proper reacting

Erotic
Treatise of sexual love

Esoteric
A few who initiates knowledge understand belonging for secret select group.

Ethiopia
Southern African Country

Existence
Being that exist mode of existing

Expression
The action of a gene, creating a protein

Extols
Praise of worship

FHEEN'_ NIX, [feen' nix]: noun. Verb: {CAMELIST' Aeroplanea}
True axis Planisphere, African hemisphere of crust structure Earth
"HART" African Continent, Devilish Girlish Figure of describing
Symbolism 9 feet 7 ½ inches Tall, Humanistic star'Realism, being
born living Habidashery of modelling Fheen'Nix the Unreal life image
of girlish figure of keratinous hairy existence and being.

Fiseco
Carnal living drive

First
Beginning class

Flirtatious
Toy with brisk move across face as smiling stealthy

Fund
Supply of money

Ge
To express language as mixing words

Ger
Gurgling sound gleefully expressed

Germ
The evolving developing living form with respect growth stage, earliest
human form.

GIBRALTAR
Network view, Saturn, the atomic star realism Needle of Development blades rings World styme image on fertility.
Note:
United States, Canada a camel living Two-hearts, South America and Africa, Styme Bow World menagerie of Holsinger.

Glibbest
Readily easy, fluent

Goody
Used to express childish pleasing

GUM
Firm tissue enveloping mass substance of waters

HABIDASHERY,   Hab'Id'-Ash'=Ery;   noun: [CAMELIST'-AEROPLANEA]
Hair realm Keratinous ruminants Cylindrical living filaments growth, keratinous coat covering the Human Head forming, fine appearing coat tuxedo appearing Haircloth, with Midwraps Biceps length, lengthy assuming slender reeling lapels, frontals: CAMELUS
Back'view with Keratinous ruminants Cylindrical living filaments growth, fine appearing Haircloth growth forming tissue of pointy appearance at the beginning crack of the TopMost of the Buttocks, CAMELISM.

Hair Follicle
A small cavity involving the epidermis and dermis skin tissue of which from dermis hair develops

Haughtiness
Proud

Hemisphere
The area with which something occurs that dominates sphere of globe

HOLSINGER, noun; verb.
Word mixture of Faith, selfconscience existing free'will, life intelligense of speaking knowledge expressing life of conscience an Mind talking pattern toward life of conscience as with this WORD that speaks conscience an being, conscience an life attribute affirming Mind life, of conscience and being, knowledgeability essentialism genetics finesse.

Humanism
Thought which human values predominate importance of views

Humanistic
Scientific humanism versed welfare

Humanitas
Human beings, the viewpoint of humankind

Hygiene
The application of scientific knowledge and practice of good health

Impulsions
Resulting state impelling the act

Individuation
Person by a name indivisible a single individuality egoism thought. Discrete existing human being

Infatuation
Characterized by absorbing desire

Ingenious
Clever

Inquisition
Curiosity eager for knowledge, One investigation being religious nature

Intraplay
Performance earnest character real life

Intravaginal
Passage leading from the Uterus to the Vulva

Jacaranda
Tropically various tree's belonging of genus: Cata.pa of genus Jacaranda family having showy clusters of usually Purplish flowers

Jadeite
Most precious type of Jade, sodium aluminum silicate, $NaAlSi2O6$.

Jade' Plant
South African Shrub, stonecrop family of Cassula argentea with small oval leaves, tasty with succulent taste.

Jazzier
Freedom ranging through the excitement, specific liveliness

Jigolo, [jig' a lo'] noun: [Zhig' a lo']
a Man whom has The earnings, gifts supported by attentions and companionship, reciprocalism returned for a Man's sexual living measure order, reciprocations from Girlish' girls behavioure acting.

Keratinous, ka rat'n as, adj.
Protein that is the insoluble outermost main constituent taught perfecting being, hair realm.

Keystone: key'ston
Selfconscience presence, Earth reflecting naked self Figurine of globe abstract cue of sweeping.

Knese: [ne's] Plural; noun, verb.
Joints giving the ability of bending connecting legs

Labeling
Describe a certain class

Labia
Skinfolds bordering the Vulva

Latte: [lat'] v.t.
Pattern spaces subset

Libertarian
A person whom maintains doctrine of "Free'=Will Living".

Light
Awareness, the aspect with which a thing appears

Linguistics
The study of language

Living
The existence active of suitability

Love: [luv] noun, verb, verb'transitive:
For the Well'Being, to embrace and Kiss

Manstar: noun
Cosmos being shining protein protonic star

Marshmallows
Light tract mass mixture of heaven*stars

Membrane
Tissue of pliable organ, serving layer thin line of Sheet material, filter, resonator, separator

Metaphysics
Cosmology existence of being

Metaphysio
Pertaining to extensive imaginative idea of philosophy

MINX
Flirtatious Girl

Modalities
Pertaining to expressing phase of form reasoning to express touch to exhibiting mood primary vision

Moisturizing
Wave appearance of mass specific cosmetic cream fondant, the air

Motile gametes
Sperm moving spontaneousness

Mudbath
Spatter with dirt the earthly matter realm, Mix wet waters

Multichanneling
Pertaining to evolving between which fresh stream passage a course of progress has

Neth
Mouth and/of Net

Neuro adsorption
Nervous system, which by utrathin layer substance one of form, surfaces substance on form being surface of another substance

Neuropath
Nerves science of feeling development

Numinous
Arousing feelings pertaining to understanding honour, realism. Realisme and loyalty

Oedipus
Lascivious, desire expressive arousing

Ontogenesis
The maturity of the individual

OOZE
To appear something

Orgasm
The experienced climax

Oxidating
Depositing substance of forms surface

Oxygen
The atmosphere and present state of pressure
Wt: 15.9994 number 8, Density 1.4290
Gravity level 0* C and 760 mm pressure

Parhelic Ring
Solar flare, self luminous solar halo of Sunlight Prismatic spray as characteristic magnetism

Periphery
Perimeter surface area external surface of a boundary

Pelvic
The bones forming this cartilaginous basin trunk

Personage
Story importance of character

Phenomenology
A thing as it appears to and is construed being constructed with the imaginative awareness that to occurrence experience itself distinguishing branch

Philosophy
Particular knowledge of doctrine attitude and truths principle of being pertaining reason guidance and proper views

Phylogenesis
The evoluting resolve of species
The evolution of the species

Physisorption
By absorption, adsorption either of the two as the organism science energy and matter form, feature exercise and force activity its living hygiene

Physiologic
The activity organic functions perform

Physiology
Pertaining to activities living the organic functions determining matter

Pie [pi] noun:
Whole easy, a layer cake and cream

Pied-a-terre [pe a'ca tar', da-, pya'] noun: plural
A residence as an apartment for part time and/of temporary use.
[French lit.,] a foct on the ground:

Pix, noun: plural
Sound film lab moving pictures

Planisphere
A map with visible use of plane on sphere

Platform
Tracks which vestible on flat surface above a stage area

Playcorner
Specific style of mechanism between the edge of space at which figure
every rectangular line angle of surface empire

Poraniour; pour eh' near: verb.
Backrinsing, wash fresh mire I, Us and of We
The essence of being

Porcelain
Vitreous translucent kaolin and feldspar with a translucent glaze

Predestinate
Purpose, act found preying heavy among value establishing view

Preface
Statement setting the acknowledging speech serving by a book

Psyche
Structure as motive of personage image of spirit, mind, Human soul

Psychosexual
Psychology equasion human sexology appearance

Pulsing Opacities
Rhythm series voltage ooze imitating light

The emulsion state applying sensitive electromagnetic globules

Putative
The view of belief good favourable acceptable usage

Quantitate
Word pertaining to measure of metrics particular stress patterns

Quark
Subatomic particle electric charge

Quiescence
Relaxing being restive at peace

RADIOIMMUNOASSAY
Transmitting measure Wave image
Imaging techniques parabolic visible X-ray embryonic method
Determining the age of the element plus its decay product

Realism
Speculative of view representing things as they really are existing

Realisme
Pertain doctrine and style experienced resemblance oneself distinguish
Pertains the experience oneself distinguish resemblance

Realists
By everyday living which figures practical life

Reciprocation
Backward and Forward

Re-examine
To examine a witness, resounding, submitting to apply over restoring
practice

Regnant
Ruling

Religiosity
Life of specific practicing fundamentalism

Responential
Living cessation, favourably answer to react by support

RNA
Ribonucleic Acid

Rotatabling
Taking place around the AXIS Traffic, Turbine of World move arrangement Textiling sanctuary existence of fundamentalism revolving mixture of class marbling 528 degrees 368 minutes

Saw
Sight and/of Seeing

Selfconscience
The expressive awareness biological life and living development human growth Mudbath Psyche emulsion regnant

Selfconsciousness
One excessively aware of One's Self own individualism by others

Semi=Fulcrum
Round half, any of various structures serving as support, Which turns moving a body

Sexologist
Of pertains to someone whom does study involving human sexual behavioures

SHINVESCARINE;** Shin' ves ka'=rein
Mixture itself creating spectacle on cloth pillar cloud cosmology existing knowledge of stars global like itself cosmology, Holsinger

Solfegio
The wuthering tones sung to ascending and descending scales
May, Me, My, Mow, Moo
Yah, Bah, Tah, Dah, Jah

Solidarity
Purpose of class point of view, between members of a group

Sponge
While absorbing various materials
The expense of certain tissue organization, Skeleton characteristics
fibrous soft particle imposing By which clean bubbling set wash

Statesmanship
An experienced political leader respected who exhibits great ability

STYME BOW
132 degree's 92 minutes
264 degree's 184 minutes
528 degree's 368 minutes
Marbling textiling by arrangement time experience of stars

Subconscious
Wholly existing which totality of mind specific
The aware assembly occurrence as speech

Superlative
Best, most, carefully and good the extreme use of greatest quantity,
intensity and quality uttermost

Supernaturalism
Shinvescarine as being Holsinger realm
Mixture image of smouldering from cosmology image ash swiftness
smart moving with speed:
GHOST pertaining to earth from Hot Sun Haloes Parhelic Rings,
fiery ash cloth smouldering worldly as darkness

Sympathectomy
Pertaining to automatic nervous system
Sympathizing thoracic and lumbar region regularity

T_Cell
T lymphocyte, T cell
White blood cell type, important nongrandular productive antibodies

Teth
Teeth

Thigh
Fatty article above of knee cap

Theoreum
Formula idea embodying statement

Tippling
Gratuity impending to excess repeatedly eager

TRIGGER, ["trig' ger"]. Noun, verb, verb transitive:
The exploding spring mechanism series, that which sensitive actuates
by act pressing when reacting to alert sphere express sequence of plane
on serious stream moving

Twilight
Revolving mean distance equating brightness from 5th dimensionalism
darkness "parabolicism'symbolism 5th dimensionalism" plane actuary
alert moving stream, fundamentalism mechanism sensitive act pressing
stream, Man Damon Ray Hollingsworth PH.D., creativity of fundamentalism

Uterine
Womb, pertaining to the Uterus

Uterus
A hollow expandable organ, which fertilized develops the egg during
pregnancy

Vagina
Where it surrounds the Vulva, a passage that leads from the Uterus

Vantage
Superiority affording strategic view

Vapours
Gaseous forms substance of fog and smoke etcetera' etcetera, etcetera

Vasocongestion
Consists of the Rhythm contractions of the extravaginal musculature
against the greatly distended circumvaginal venous plexi and vestibular
bulbs in the outer third of the vagina

Vasomotor
Regulating certain nerves as the Diameter of blood vessels

Venous Plexous
Pulmonary artery cf nerves as the Diameter network structure

Voluptuous
Gratifying senses characterized pleasure and sensous enjoyment

Vulva
Genitalia, external female organ passage affording the Uterus strategic
view

Wash
Cleansing spiritualism by acting waters moistening flows force of form
carrying spirit'flesh, being human physics flesh, that being spiritualism,
wash and wear the World goes around fast.

Wax
Hydrocarbons, carbons, glycerines, CO_2's, NcO_2's

Whisp
Delicate as smoke

XX
Moreover reactance applied magnifying variable of sexually applied
gene

XY
Characterized gene of magnifying sexually applied variable

YE
You

YEA
Yes

Yeah
Yes

Yearn
Long desire an feeling tenderness moving honest concerns

YEP
Yes

YES
Reply affirmative an give assent the approval

To express statement the "Okay"

Zest
Keen, hearty, agreeable an Charming

ZISTENSE; zis' tens: noun, verb, transitive verb:
Charm, pertains to exist
The activity of feeling
The electro' energy alternating with fermentation

Zoom
The act moving sharply with speed

Humanistic Sexologist
Theoreum [1]

Quantitate Existence Of Quark

Scholars development creating knowledge itself fundamentalism, Method take arts thought teaching work the evolcting network revolving.

Where a key various time atmospheric calling the attractive activity only at the existing tapestry view, world hemisphere image of star textiling the image each princ.pal living judgement, creativity appears calling figure of star rhythm mixture axis plane around wandering light 264 degree's 184 minutes marbling textiling by arrangement. Mixture image of class sanctuary existence of fundamentalism revolving, development styling Gib'Ral'-Tar, rhythm houses world hemisphere impressive image of styling Gib'Ral'-Tar, creativity appears calling figure of styling Pell'=Mell. light techniques systematic view of star. Responsibility awarding dirt may appear representing gravels specific voicing vast here experience airing breadth breathe of gravel landmark. mountain sweet practice of development by art.stic course of Styme Bow World Holsinger Rock, keystone of faith physically understanding planet architectuary around wandering light, time it has Museum development sanctuary activity of Sunlight thou, sand, bridge and stand the exciting same activity of Sunlight time atmospheric world life arrangement where a view with good documenting Gib'Ral'-Tar realm tapestry mixture atmospheric. Creativity appears calling figure of star rebuilt cultural life everyday around judgement.

My name is Damon Ray Hollingsworth
I am this planet physical living Gibraltar
Holsinger rock, keystone is roof, Faith Holsinger
My name is Gib'Ral'-Tar
I am this planet physical living Styme Bow

World   Holsinger   Ministries   Limited   SHINVESCARINE   of Heaven.

Forever came to stay!

Damon Ray Hollingsworth PH.D.

Games

Enjoy yourself
Jacks, Checkers, Marbles, Chess, Cards
Tonk, Pinochle, Bid-whisk, Koon kan, Rummy
Hearts, Poker, 7-Up, Black Jack, Spades
And Gin again:
These games, We've played varies to Handball, Softball
Soccer, Boxing, Basketball, Baseball, Football, Hockey
At the Ball, The Masquerade is for, only a very select few
And those adored, Played Tennis too…

Damon Ray Hollingsworth PH.D.

Playcorner' Movement

The Playcorner movement, Fun, refreshing muscles, heart and lungs body alignment, cardiovascular conditioning and strength training. Basic movements purchase this stair'step, class stationary window the intelligense of forms humanism, the quality of being human of thought and/or actions based on nature, interests and ideals of man, specifically a rationalist movement that holds man is capable of self=fulfillment, ethical conduct etcetera with recourse to Supernaturalism having considered what are the best qualities of human beings, kind, tender, merciful, sympathetic belonging to and typical of man, devoted to promoting good welfare of humanitas sculpture, observant flesh bread customary apple honey'sweet figure and flower. Desperado acknowledge it, We've got to find the treasury, Marshmallows moisturizing, You might think, you might say something? Something you might understand! Might lives on mercy, marshmallows.

Should you think and say?

Life and life is light, tis Moon desperado marshmallow.

Desperado a piece of the Sky, knowledge of noise obey rising my own drum perspective=ass, coloures of Sun, stars time a airplane a flying that mind you, marshmallows parhelic ring.

Thee important thing is that she is a living girl all of a living girl to think of. Whom of flesh and bone aegis her own humanism upon humanist living, Okay!

How do you explain love? And you work and you love.

Um, what you're "eh" doing now, activity is growth, which life is, by exciting somebody you want to make exciting, You want to make exciting ceremonies, YAH' YAH:

Life explains love, If, we explain because, Okay' we love!

Explain, why we're simply here. Okay!

Because, she has the lips of a big mouth Bass.

You ever been Kissed by a big mouth Bass?

From ear to ear, it twill get your lobes wet, like a smiling Barracuda we're here.

Dialogue:

Manstar:	Am I mistaken—Your eyes look alittle bit moist like you are about to cry a something.
Girlish Figure:	You mean: [eyes, they raise] they raise?
Manstar:	Yes
Girlish Figure:	I felt perhaps that, We two sit on the inside in the middle.
Manstar:	Umm Hmm, I have lots of things to do
Girlish Figure:	What have you got to do?
	Sometimes I want to do, except, I want to do something!
Manstar:	You talk so fast, do you always "wooh" talk that fast?
Girlish Figure:	Always, Oh Boy:
	Giggling with a flirtatious way, she moves toward him, and sits back on her chair, she flays her legs wide spread, tilts her head, puts her hands on her hips with geature of conversation and gauges active autistic looks flirtatious, ["WOWR"].
Girlish Figure:	WOWRrRr, How do you feel?
Manstar:	Fresh

Girlish Figure: You do? You just did? Tell me, do you feel love?

Do you love?

Metaphysio "eh" hygiene of biosynthesis vapours shadow mass tissue extension knowledge upon metaphysics cells nerve of mass fibers synthesis bio, Appropos curiosity a house is a home and "eh" home is just a place "eh" too layer your stuff.

Doctor of Divinity, Independent Bishop Damon Ray Hollingsworth
PH.D.

Humanistic Sexologist Theoreum [2]

Introduction, Creative Expression

Beyond Dreams, Creative expressions maximize accuracy as science understanding craft that create a perception knowledgeable, approaching human convection life of dwelling being, therewith good scouring body of existence appearance of species. The aesthet_cism doctrine aesthetic, sensitivity and beauty, what considering desire eminent numinous knowledge of understanding. By which means peace and prosperity of continuation subconscious glibbest fashion. Femme [fem, fam] noun plural Femmes [femz] Superlative expressing the greatest degree, attribute expressed human nature and mixture erect figuring girlish development. Human female convection designating having a hollow particle approach shaped to receive a corresponding inserted sheath [called"male"]. Human female convection designating of a reproductive structure and containing large gametes [eggs] that can be fertilized by smaller motile gametes [sperm].

This female sexual drive, activity and state of quantuum being, Ho'=and/of Hole

Mo'=and/of More and Mow "meaning to Overwhelm" Membra and Genitalia, vulva and the uterus vaginal structure attributed positive attribute expressing Homosexuality, open membrane of cavity affluence, aye' natural born woman, female Oedipus birth constriction. You see a man seeing, acknowledges a girlish vagina and says HO'=MO'=and He acknowledges that plain sight of seeing the Hole as He indulges himself fantasy with this Hole attributing He see's the Hole and tries to fill it up with his Penis, which is where it is being called "SEX'=U'=ALL", Why?

Why, which is he is trying the ANUS and her MOUTH, thee Oedipus complex true is birth constriction.

The more interesting question is, where is Homosexuality?

Where does Homosexuality stand?

What do I believe? I know what I believe, between the vulva and the uterus canal, vaginal structure and the outer third of the vagina and the labia and clitoridal area with sex, HO'=and/of HOLE an MO'=and/of MORE and "MOW" meaning to Overwhelm, methods cells bacterium vagina intravaginal labeling.

Thus the union, human hole and the intercourse inserted by union, there apt, the image at which where is specifically Vulva and the Uterus structure, it vagina is true a Hole' an More' of, Sex'=U'=All, living Ho'=Mo'=Sex'=U'=All. Love and various human desire of variety aesthetic preponderance idea and kindling the essay assessment spasticity witness concrete attainment, percutaneous claudication, venous plexus vasomotor, sympathectomy, cerebrovascular, cardiovascular, bio-chronic neuro adsorption, Physisorption, absorption neuropath mante act "DNA" of bacterium "RNA" its series form "T" Cells putative accelerating, Holsinger, come "eh" Holy Ghost them love idea and Hart. What fruits I am glad to say, whom to reason to say, give I, My Thanks, demographic needs doctrinaire epidermis platform, RadioImmunoassay, who are anyone and to do, something not to who also, I love and love it meant loved so much.

The eastbound, story opportunity anyone who are everyone

The south, volunteer what is truly with that they service to. The west, you did too one of we've acute any given change accounting severity whereabouts.

The north, answer just one question? Would they be so hot, what strikes bare, strikes bottom, between me one existence officially yard cousins. Yet, what paint there is droops middle of being happiness, human discovery you share.

So, why would you pick the wrong team, when you know what the outcome is going to be! When you know all the long that its been recorded history that you can't win and you know in the first place without even having to sit on the side and watch to see what the outcome is going to be, cause you already know and whether or not you're knowledgeable of it. You know it, in your mind and sometimes because, you're knowledgeable of something in your mind, whether or not you know it. You walk that walk and you talk that talk.

Self preservation is the first law of nature, Survival is of the fittest. Whether or not you read it or you know it, you know it, in your mind! That's why survival is of the fittest, so, you walk that walk and you talk that talk. Self preservation is the first law of nature!

You got life Fucked'Up, You Bitch.

The ability to love, share and care, I'd like to think like that credibility, sanctity of doctrine on fertility. One voice like a racing heart, as I that is guide experience that graces weakness to hide behinds. The enclosure of view for reason both terms virtue and charcoals smells. Perhaps you should read naked knowledge and its claim buy, upon this timeout, that she seduced me, We among mud Hello your Ass, post age handling, true love: Plea'=B: Merchants'=C

Gamble I'm walk, we imagined much to experience "Apathy" sense earned. You know everytime, you go out on the "street" space of time in so to speak of intellect you spend time, which is to realize someone who knowledge it is thee understanding of admission that with the things of it and/of something with this, bearing the existence of pursuit the active ability of characterizing things living knows.

A. The Clitoral Orgasm

B. Vaginal Orgasmic Jump Peak

Fact that Muscular Vulval rolling climactic release undertones sensitive of being, pleasurability of beauty. When you luv someone and you think you're holding on to tight, there should be no acknowledgeable known reason to doubt you.

Much Luv, DIABLO
Damon Ray Hollingsworth PH.D.

Poem

A wise Man governs, his voluptuous impulses
Laugh, laughter, laughing
Whilst sitting on the side of the bed
Sighing, crying, these Words I pondered, these
Words I said
Such s a Kiss so-called, be one up and Opulent
Quite different from the fall…

Key To Pronunciation

Long Vowels and Dipthongs

[Accented syllables, the sounds expressed by {a} in Marriage is a long vowel, and (i) in Mine is a dipthong.]

Sound	Examples	Pronunciation
a as in are	Star, Car	star, kar
::: air	Air	ar
a:::[1] fate	name, gain, reign, plane	nɛm, gan, ran, plan
[2] fair	stare, care	star, kar
a::: Castle [long or short]	ask, task, bath, pass	ask, task, bath pas
e:::[1] me	seed, scene, deed, clean	sed, sɛn, ded, klen
[2] dear	cheer, peer, clear	cher, per, kler
e as in fern	term, heard, firm	term, nerd, ferm
i as in mind	quite, light, sight	quit, lir, sit
[1] fire	inquire, sire, lyre	in kwair, sir, lir
o as in mote	pole, boat	pol, bot
::: [1] more	score, floor	skɔr, for
o as in form	warm	worm
u as in mute	cute, dew, suit	kut, du, sut
::: [1] curious	pure, endure	pur, en-dur'
u as in turn	word, burn	wurd, ɔurn
oo::[1] Moor	moot	moot
:::: [2] Moon	loom	loom

[y]oo as in super

[u or oo]	assume, lure	a-s{y}oom, l{y}oor
aw :::: saw	daub, dawn, law, all	dawb, dawn, law, awl
ow :::: now	found, house	fownd, hows
oi :::: Toy	oil, boy	oil, boi

Short Vowels

Sound	Examples	Pronunciation
a as in sat	mat	mat
e ::::: bed	read, head, said	red, hed, sed
i ::::: bid	him, hymn	him, him
o ::::: hot	knock	nok
u ::::: bud	sung, son	sung, sun
oo :::: good	book, cook	book, cook

Vowels of Unaccented Syllables

Sound	Examples	Pronunciation
a as in Signal	withal, verdant, mental	wiTH al', ver'dant, men'tal
::: [1] alter	alter	awlt' ar
e as in moment	potent	po' tent
::: [1] silver	clever	klev' er
::: [2] parish	minute, mountain, merit, lily	min'it, mownt'in mer'it, lil'i
O ::[1] bishop	abbot, aloft	ab'ot, a-loft'
::: [2] rigour	author, sailor	awth'or, sal'or
u :: [1] circus	cretaceous, nimbus	kre-ta'shus, nim'bus
::: [2] figure		
::: [3] tenure	adventure	ad-ven'tyur

Note:

The pronunciation given for words are the traditional ones used throughout present modern day influence on literature and learning. These words and phrases in their pronunciation, now regarded as being that of the present modern fundamentalism.

Consonants

Sound			Examples	Pronunciation
ch	as in	cheap	feature	fe'tyur
f	:::	fell	fate, phone, laugh	fat, fon, laf
g	:::	guard	game, mitigate, good	gam, mit'i-gat, good
Gw	:::	linguist	penguin	peng'gwin
gz	:::	exist	example	egz-am'pl
H	:::	loch	pibroch	pe'broH
hw	:::	wharf	wheat	hwet
j	:::	jewel	just, jade, gentle, rigid	just, jad, jen'tl rij'id
k	:::	cold	kite, keel	kit, kel
ks	:::	explain	relax	ri-laks'
Kw	:::	quite	queen, choir	kwen, kwir
ng	:::	longer	rang, rank, sing	rang, rangk, sing
s	:::	see	sole, cede, scent	sol, seed, sent
sh	:::	machine	shape, shine, pressure sugar, mention, precious	shap, shin, presh'ur, shoog'ar, men'sh(o)n, presh'us
th	:::	health	theme	them
TH	:::	then	bathe, clothe	bath, kloTH
y	:::	feature	young, yet, super	yung, yet, s(y)oo'per
z	:::	zone	zest, muse, maze, cruise	zest, muz, maz, krooz
zh	:::	azure	vision, measure, bourgeosie	vizh'(o)n, mezh'ur, boorzh'-wa-ze

NOTE:

Fundamentalism, being present literature and learning, glibbest phrases their Modern day influence on words.

Gum

Transmitting sounds quietly resembling a soft and gentle, "rain storm" transpiring with the echoing sound of a "water fall" and in the exact duplication of a "raging thunder storm" in pride of "watery" soft droplets of "raining water" and "rain". Releasing a continually "immaculate wind" transmitting the sound in form of actual expression as:

SSssssHh, SSSSsssssHHHhhh, SSsSssHhHHHhh, HAH, HaH, SSSssHhH, Hah, Hah, SSSsHh, SssHh, SSSsssssHHHhhhh, Hah, Hah, Hah, HAH, HAH, Hah, SSSSsssssHHHh, SSSSssHhhH Grime, the World goes around fast, twirls on its Axis, "AXIS" shimmering brilliant white soft and gentle a spark of light, stars light the night darkness, SSsssHhSH, SSSssHhSH, SssSsHhSH, ShAZzzzzzzzzzz brushing through the tree's and the leaves on the tree branches, being nestled in the breezes of the falling winds flap with the air currents creating the sounds "pronounced" "[Glass: Glass]" "[Gliss: Glass]". Packman nitroglycerine, tumbling moments of display with thunder and lighting sonic booming, sometimes cool winds the humidity fleeting semi'independent structure, the humidity grappling display of moment window through the tree's, rustling the tree branches and wrestling through the leaves, creating thus sounds "coo'=waite'=trick'-crinkel'=crinkel" Wet as these are of being firmament waters, with all of their contents seeing firm, being true and the immaculate existent firmament. Boiled and splashed around by ash living clouds the existent fire and rinsed and dried through the immaculate winds of change, existence, releasing that constant sound transmitting the echo expressive of SSSSsssssHHhSH, SSSsssHhSh, SSSsssHHhShH, SSsssHhhH, HAH, HAH, SSSSsssssHHhhHShH, HAH, HAH, HAH Voicing repeatedly constant verbalizations sylla-

23

bles sounding as if though drinking. GE: GER: with a transpiring sound being transmitted of physical existence appearing as thee sudden "wash" of a sudden fast rain storm with the echoing sound that is transmitted with the illustration of some of its "immaculate substance" and goes. Splat, Splat, Splat, Splat, Splat, Splat, Splat, real sudden and fast: Latte, Latte, Latte, Latte, Latte, Latte, Latte, Latte, Latte, Latte:

Types of clouds, meaning "[Claus]" cause of acting, Cirrus, Cumulus, Stratus, Nimbus:

Memories of Diablo as work maintainance environmentalism rendezvous Damon Ray Hollingsworth PH.D.

Words Of Worth

So many nice things to do with space an time

And yet, some are still dreams and some are still true.

Desire fills the heart of thine faithful of whom is thee fire of love, built for humanity and cresting through shadows eternities, Words of worth, human favour, self-discovery.

Treasure islands, moving stars celibacy and Shinvescarine of Heaven, Holsinger sings.

Damon Ray Hollingsworth PH.D.

The Simplicity of Shame

The Simplicity of Shame is the shallow shadow of sorrow
    Thee Simplicity of love, desirous a feeling of being.
    Out of this stance, out of this understand you see
    Now I see with being, to just plain live.
    That this is an realizing, You respond thus your estimation
    and you will see to just plain live.
    Thee Simplicity of Sorrow, of envy!

This that I have to say of the most living desire, the desire of lust. Sorrow is the shadow of desire, thee simplicity of shame!

The Simplicity of shame is the shallow shadow of sorrow, the simplicity of love desirous a feeling of being to existing the existence, a great simplicity with an abundance of feeling for silence.

You must see thee struggling with a heavy rain perfuming fragrance, moving clouds.

Out of this stance, out of this understand, you see that this is an realizing you respond which means there is, Now I see with being falling in the groove of innocence. It is in the state of infinite space, in your estimation and you will see, it to exist that's just toward plain living, live existence.

Thee Simplicity of Shame its bounds to have and to be as well as cures for maintainance irony openwork scope architectury on life of cloud triggering, I am brainchild mixed up with the bones and front Hart Lub=Dup coil life "eh" coitus cup ooze and slime, I want to acknowledge "eh" with my life. And hugs and squeezes of a feeling for being humanistic sexualism.

Thee Simplicity of Shame is a great simplicity with an abundance of feeling for silence, individuum not the acknowledging works, and not the acknowledgings system with, Don't do what will make you sorry! Don't say, what you do not mean! If, You can't say sumpthing with "Good'measure" and "Treasure it to being" then don't say any got damn thing, to understanding thoughts.

To Understanding Thought, My Heart goes out to You!

Independent Bishop, Damon Ray Hollingsworth PH.D., Doctor of Divinity and Pastoral Counselor Diplomaed and Doctor of Biblical Counseling.

Humanistic Sexologist Theoreum [3]

Chapter 1
The Man's Standards

Venous Plexus Vasomotor Sympathectomy "Aeroplanea" oxygen mante ooze and coil light triggering, A Man's Sex is what he is

Those that are flesh doeth mind, to the things that are flesh:

A Man is what his sex is, living socioeconomics tremendous right paid fundamentalism starring fiseco aeroplanea, eyes tippling.

This movement may express, itself, the same movement underneath the movement to find out what truth is…!

You this movement to find out what is real, what is truth, what is love, You want the name that you bare to be known and to continue through guarantees. Do you ever go out, for a walk by yourself?

It is very important to go out alone, to sit under a tree, by yourself and observe the falling of a leaf, hear the splash and running of the water with the dust of rain on dry land, watch the flight of a bird and of your own thoughts? Watch your own thoughts, watch these things out of this stance, you see, your own thoughts chase each other across the space of your mind.

If you are of this motion to be alone and watch these things and see the darkness wave, then you will discover which is the movement of being realtime, darkness wave across space what you have as you are understanding realism, matters, dwelling time and chance, eyes'tippling love. Aeroplanea assuming ruminants because I want what you have! Because I want as you are, I want with what I am, I want you, You see I am love envious. I am envious because I want what you have!

I am envious because I want with what I am, you see I am, I want as you are I want you love.

Love is being envious, dwelling time and chance eyes'tippling.

Insatiably curious a student, writings were expressions statuesque envy, Envious the picturesque ardent joy of living struggling to shape in letters a life and a living by fancying themselves of prose and Blank'-verse, free form metre and rhymes, projection of feeling with the passages times, Reading stanza, key tie lines:

Teth'=Neth'=Babb'=Ye'=Back'=Thigh'=Knese, Baby I love Ya, Baby I will marry Yah, Baby I got a habit, right now, I'm a little to shy.

Just once, I'd like to tell you that all my dreams will blind you and you'd know it. Baby you should think of me, like you shouldn't and you'd know I walk alone.

You may find, if, you think you can walk in and back out of my life any time, you want. Yet, that does not justify, that I should agree and I can only thank the Lord. You see life, the intimidable mounting, I've surmised it is the summit. You seek apt insofar convenient, arranged within thus to need, appear near toward your convenience exposed inclusion, just as on a colour wheel thee shadings we conventionally name Yellow and Black have around them infinite gradations of colour. I have had two-aims, first to make them fully in content, second to write them with clear precise appropriation. Perhaps all of this presages, perhaps? Baby, it is my intentions to meet the needs of Baby! Baby, I wish you to give it to me straight, Thus a friend…

Love, thee statement translation, manuscript of that reaction a reply and dwelling that time in an essay, that defense contrasting analytic reason describing the expression of imagination the arts improvement of man by opening his mind and freshness to things. Which minister to all things to loveliness it marries under its light moving within thereof radiance of its presence which it breathes, it strips that veil of familiarity of this world and lays bare the naked and sleeping.

When life being aware of itself has awareness of its fellow human of the possibilities of its future, this awareness of its own life span, death writing this living. This awareness of human separation, reasons, so, he moves from this love of a lady to a love of which makes her, by whose means his imagination realizing she actually is the soul aroused thereby his mind and vicarious discourse without veil of cloud views. Moves love-led beyond senses thus sea of pure divine and receives it into himself and enjoys dry light of reason, the heart of realism.

He receives that kiss, which is a joining of souls, he seeks to enjoy seeing and hearing this girl, to train her mind and thus small things, he is stirred to enjoy with delicacy as being toward delight toward rejoicing toward pleasure, seeking bodily possession a certain far off perfume. Minds find individuals, only individuals do impress themselves upon the eyes, the ears, upon any of our senses. Individuals are an intuitions guide and the individualism being the intuition of the senses, whereas concepts them the mind makes by its action on the intuitions of sense. Thus mind devises the abstractions which it uses true with the arts diverse multitudes in allegiance and employments. These as sentiments thus perceptions, the expressions wave are a wave on a rising tide upon man's absolute and totalism therewith the obedience, criterion of sex.

Criterion of sex, thereby with sexualism thus sexual drives putative facts portrays man as a being of whom needs and powers holds that the growth of man's range his needs can expand reason, right reason.

Reason stems the intent the instance, "Two'Lungs" it allows within that species variabilities provocative of needs. A genetic human engineering that true impinge on a preliminary description of depth, "Biogenetic'Law".

Ontogenesis, the maturation of the "id" the individualism

Phylogenesis, the evoluting revolving, the evolving thereof species Involving the additional pathology of the "RNA" and the "DNA" a movement of "Adrenaline" with a pathology of 'Adrenaline" to, its being that system to fill in the growth involving adrenaline flows.

Through this light brought thereas "Thesis" X's long standing, feeling of making Y aware of X's acts of feeling of Y's fixating the analysis that has an important consequence is fundamental childishness, "Boy's and/of Girls". Man draws by an large of most human determinants of emphasis thought weighs on scale of morale and the importance an a way with which man interacts with the rest of reality in structuring and restructuring his civilization. One instance, civilization construing man's bacteriology impelling him to work as a response to the require-ment to fulfill a given instance often rich extensive fulfillment of man in response to his amazing effect "Thesis" human desire. Through the enhancement, this writing, which the enrichment thereby enriches the vocabulary of economics with these expressions taught being thereof philosophy, that jargon of various disciplines, the materialist concep-tion of "class" and "capital" [phenomenology of soul] Man and the "bacteriology of man" of human construct finding.

If you "Fucken", you're Married! You can't have [sex] unless, You can be married. If you can't be married, you can't have sex! That's called "Compatibility and Suitability". If you having "SEX" you're married.

Chapter 2
The Deepest Need of Mankind

Of all the systems to rationalize the romantic reaction, the fast bound substance of the revealing garment of the sky, that makes the attribute of nearness actual to the light of men, withstanding lay whereinto a man's eyes. The nearest, clearest, nearest warmest symbolism being these often bound their human psyche, richness of selfconscience. You submit because you as a person a moment within totality, its deep depths and treasures, moves its predestined way on its own energy.

They start their life together with a visit to a wine cellar and they move on to the kitchen, in terms of personal history, is thee student bored with books? This fullness a genuine love and attainment.

Waiting, he catches sight in a mirror of the girls face and figure, shining he is rapt and cannot withdraw his eyes. We see him the waterfall upon whose foaming spray the Sun paints a rainbow, reality is desire. Movements drew and held, movements to apply only a drawn realism movements drew and held near. To her heart the reality was personal, it was a dominant theme real enough in itself futilities of living passing attention she employed with equal ease and freedom of making her medium the instrument of his intent. He knew, how much personal disposition and individual experience determine alike the shapes on love and the shapes of love and the love which impels the imagination, he speculates just to look at her. He speculates on how he would have bathed? Just to look at her wherein is serenity of soul and herein is the height of love, embodiment thereinto ideals this stretch of feelings, feeling impelling a girls heart. The girls of art, so, so, so conveys that to feel that which proves idealist representation of works of art of man, so, to multiply the availability of all things and exalt the dignity of man! When you realize absolute insight of a living thing, in its light allaying by the subtle dabblings by the subtle mind of dab-blings, So, so, feeling tinting of the desire to living a strand of the changing climates, quite then the achievements of statesmanship, states of the mind chance impression, we then call them ideals, images and prezoom they are what conveys most concerned with.

The Man and his ideas were attractive enough in that time to Win him a seat of the assembly. There he stood to the voice he launched brought to direct calling to a life of living thought. You can in pure and objective vision practice realism thereby your art is real, its practice realism and its Theoreum to apply doctrines movements to state that which discerns the feeling with this works deep psyche.

The intraplay between them and you reveals the soul of thine age, image and postulation and this soul is a moment in the predestinate time, which manifest itself. Consoling herself with man in the face of academic copyright, marriage a vision a map of life more pat to the soul and the times she found the vision bearing with and held unchanging to her allegiance, the scene in the window casting the shadow of that in the grip of reaction of living men and women, con-spiring to loving, loyal understanding and enduring passions, which live with thoughts stood by, which is made flesh and walks on this World as parents, teachers, chancellors, soldiers, preachers, justified themselves, mankind thus thereinto a vision of the universe and cos-mos being planted life on this world plauditing mankind into a vision of the world and man and destiny unique to fruition what in seed, the prophet of freedom and love, defining the intent of those of being that loving heart and free soul of the world winning free at last figures of Hella's instruments of the soul.

We seem nevertheless more imaginative and not being able to free ourselves of the necessity to think beyond spatial modalities, doctrines and disciplines we acquiesce of the familial system of mystic melodies, which heal and purify feelings, somehow relaxing, purifies, lightens and delights men's souls. With man's discipline, direction though driven by impulse as whim prompts, were adrift during a willfulness of joy and bliss and freedom. The epitome of the lives of many and this existence, mere existence, regardless of its quality is better and more to be desired than non-existence, which existence can yield and is so satisfied with living. It is an act instantaneous Wellspring of enchanneling a life of feeling. New costumes, new scenes, new light and shading and passion straight flaming at heart and eyes. In setting forth my ideas about its future sprinklings of intravention into human tentative controversial subject, a particular point of view of the path of movement to attempt a thoughtful concern with the destiny of the familial is made manifest by man's emerging mind.

At length, my view of tentative principles, concerning indications and contraindications, I shall point the way to the special values of this procedure. I shall reflect on the questions of the text and context on the human condition of our time, with special concern for the relation between familial change and familial health viewed by the light of familial practice of structure and strength, real labour realm that yields a benchmark long terms spread of globe ownership.

The solidarity of this word sweeping the world of personality and the quest for the recognition of the link induced by the recognition of familial living. In this setting the consequence to our time, the continuity of the institution of the familial, the real issue is the human condition. Through this quest, we envitably allot they either recognize each movement living work with depth realities of living, drawn nearing back thereinto at that deep phase of direct concern by this movement on the face of this human condition during space of that deep timing it stirs living individuation it merges fond striving humanist consequences to adjust personality to environment by adherents to extol an audience there onto view man's descriptive parlayance of parlaying place of familial labours. Ongoing this viewing, this seems knowledge upbeat touching gracious lines with this field of periphery, my conceptualizations that reconceptualize to conceptualize the familials picturesque ardent view. Picture a familial visiting, visiting you and thus this your own home. Think about the way they make an entrance entering the room, the especial ways different of saying, Hello; most reassuring their differentialisms reconceptualizing kinds of handshakes. Then reconceptualize the mechanistic mechanisms of this flow of netherworld reacting. Think of your own family for just one moment, your own family has moments at which on familial stability as this system. It is interesting to notice at note, I think a sense of timing that will give us seemingly honest more of a capacity of capstone atonement talking in a way that reveals sequential familial happenings describing growth. Familial structure and thereby human sequential fundamentalism human the environment is so, that fundamental structures are a point of being the equilibrium nearby on the understanding growth and change and the ability attitudes compiling desired activity artistic cherishing, clandestine own properties.

Familial is a special method of treatment of a primary and fondling group structure. It is a procedure eschews, that, make and the usage of a true group. With that thought being of familiarity with this group of a familial uniting. Thus it points toward developing ways, means of giving help through this neverending concourse of needs for the individualisms brought to certain methods of maintainance.

When a family recognizes intellectuality intellectually, intellectualisms and feels the emotionality eschewing that these involving tie lines are pertinent to witticisms.

What I have to say is to an extent I realize human and intuitive vantage, "[Subjective Construct'Finding"]". With certainty, ascertaining families themselves, certainty of families their activities and their ways of referring to themselves always imply a "WE". Most parents refer random characterizings toward bringing light musings gesturing that child, this boy, them children, my kids. According to acknowledging a structure of class the amusement first given, visualized as a lineage an linkage around line aesthetics drawn to embodying reconceptualizing modes of feeling to understand structure of familiarity of familial mante ecosystem. We are here of mankind, epic of lives arts live on with this world which lives on through stage of plays, of styles, which is right need and due altercatings psychosexualisms, multichanneling a continuous system building strategy of what cosmology ecosystem drumming drum, drums.

ETHIOPIAN' MOON

Harvesting growth, transparently animalism response and scripting voice is starry'art. State of dreams vast web cry with deep throat feature interfacing realism that this developing package, art, work keystone of camelist'camelus, camelism world dreams; Moon, a you give interfacing features. State of dreams represent time is telescopic cue it freeze as snow windows sky. You much more after, representing graphical live on world web rolling ground pleasure of Moon, a as may it please. Art, Hot Sun [Hah' Sun] charge on premier realm, planetarium beauty wraps same availability you may use it still.

Chapter 3
Equasion of Living Bacterium

Girl, indelibly created by Faith, especially of Man

The right passive affect is the active concern that love is a standing with.

Realization of that fact, Wind'swept through yonder distances, I'm shure I am shure, finding you curious thee Art of loving.

On stocks and stones jostling rocks, chosen you, here are the two of us, museum of a human psyche taught that this world, thee humanization of man. Personage regnant context of this rock and wave of cloud and storm, a wide audience undoubtably including thee students of young girls finishing schools. Stating: AH, OOH, HMMMmmmmmmmM, UNH: HAH, HAH, HAH, HAH, HAH, HAH, HAH, HA; stretching backward through space a fields width outward surrounding all directions, and this Art, it is a thing Miraculous. In each, we can point to why this thing is thought to express feeling, status of which we recognize of furthering this fact of projecting a mystic chill, first numbing dependence of feelings upon minds attitude.

Her heart, was all that thee actual loveliness was, Living figures of flesh and bone, each individualism and unique its humanism.

This humanist spread, a burning up of all feeling, the dry light of reason. Personality, he knew is feeling and this girl, he knew with small degree, tinting by accoutrements the art flows.

Love is the most practical thing that this world has given toward human beings. To love, to be kind, to be applicable influencing, to think for yourself. These are all very practical things and they will bring about a practicality of standing alone and thinking this awareness with your heart and mind, with ones own seriousness, which we have learnt through writing, through drink, a few words occur here and there thesis flourishings, and it is thereby announcement through hidden things of your mind, we are young to be in an environment.

We are young to be in an environment, the haughtiness of a Man, stopping to observe this tide as worshipping Sunlight and this Paradise of being Moonlight, rolling westward as it grows dark. The automatic stars, fermenting watch, to guide understanding, what you exist from moment to moment that you worry about a behavioural state of learning. Life is stealthy understanding and learning taught with species knowledge of facts, sex, play, work'guidance of works, love and truth. Consistence is when there is a sense of love and your own desires want you to be identified, a mind that is watching thoroughly of moment, you say? I have discovered I know I am, because I have found being the existing state existence assures life equasion bacterial living, humanist mankind.

What you say? How you talk? How you walk? How you look at the skies, all things are important, because they act like mirrors that show you as you exist. You are as your well-being and screen to idiosyncrasies, you soon discover everything anew, from moment, moment to moment, HAHN.

Then Man of girls, that's the equasion of living bacterium, the important thing is that she is a living girl all of a living girl to think of whom of flesh and bone upon humanistics her own humanism upon humanistic living.

You show to this man, whom has nothing to give you, let us work, tell me what to do, and by understanding that, he will come to understand himself by which he lives, helps him to do so, and by understanding that to as this interpretation of what I have said. If you want to travel light, if you want to climb to a great height, You must travel light.

Perhaps, you think and think over these matters? Yet, you must awake to everything, which you, perhaps, which may be somewhat this world on which all of us have existing properties that livelihood scouring transient knowledge. Do you understand? We are non-binding, yet, we also exist living World Styme Bow'Winkle and calling we all have acceptance of coursing Shinvescarine. You may talk about simplicities? What I am talking about there can be only existing "Multiplication of Shadows". Yet, there is just the Oneness, "Won" realisms reality and it is this spirit that Ghosting' Ghost that is the importance, important. To acknowledge, existing how ones mind works is a base effort twining guarantees purpose of education. Now, watch there, out of this the awareness to you, the arisings love awakenings with your heart. You and I must understand this to, it ourselves and then, we shall discover just what it is of that what we call life. Love will arise of your heart, when you have acceptance as that which may bring about the exchange of what reflective block to condense thus identify yourself and another, when you meet and observe without judging, just the observance, observe.

You see, I have tried not talking to find just what happens if I don't talk. That is alright too. Do you understand? If there is love, if you have assured love within your heart and your heart is knowledgeable accounting the awareness with things that love is living bound not with things of the mind, then it is like a fountain, like a wellspring that is timelessly giving fresh waters. Which is the acute activity of perfuming a performance of perfume of this breadth of living.

Now, you and I have to understand this, it is a Young Man, who is asking this question. Do you know, what it means to love somebody?

Do you? Do you know, what it means to love, so that you take care of it, feed it, cherish it, though it may give you nothing in return, though it may depend on you, which implies this that wants to be loved? Do you understand? Do you just understand what love is? And your own desires want you to be identified and whom therefore acknowledging what love is?

It is alone to plant on a path trodden stone, by many a bare feet.

When the Hills call, you will follow. If you love something, you never get tired of it. I mean love with which there is no seeking of a result, no wanting something from it. When you love something, it is not self-fulfillment, therefore there is no disappointment, there is no end. Why am I doing this? You might as well ask, why does a rose bloom? Why does Jasmine give its scent? And, why do birds fly?

To know how to think is easy, yet, to know just what to think, requires a great deal of constituencies amicably accounting contentment and the understanding through this motive of constant movement of some backwater of life. And, is of seeing what is from moment to moment without wanting to exchange it, Now, You and I have understanding, to understand this with that very perception. You know, it is very interesting to find out, what we call thinking is the absolute of response of memory, any contact with reality at large as that sense of peace, we retain that sense to have the exciting same acting kindness, feeling an the experience of joy, that sense of peace, we, retain this rememberance of all that from which there is, what we call thinking. This and to love on a peaceful morning, yet all the time at times, it is the service of a man to respond one way his own dominance aggressivness to. And to view the justification human bacterium stresses complete orgasmic touch, we perceive each our ability to see, to touch, to hear, worth presence of permissive exhaustion pleasuring to afford give=to=get, there accentuating there "eh" will be orgasm vaginal distinction modes that belong that contribute experiencing coitus most human beings diversity of psychological varyings true amount derived between consummating presence equable arousal with desires sweltering human meanderings which becomes submerged needs virtual love, union delights welfare a ritual living making love.

The existing mere experience, acting bespeaks beloved being bestowal loving feeling. Semi=fulcrum of pleasurability of specific chartist movement humanity accompanies real world romanticism. Lover's need and beloved's welfare, it, is describing, transcend desire ardent bacterium, perceptive one and to say, which is true apparent truism, we are taught that to as the act take us beyond depths sex, being was made. Attitude acknowledges knowledge ultimately and thoroughly as selected of mankind, Thus cling that understanding elicit with choice. Choice experiences coital love as love of stock responses bacterium to series.

This love itself modernism sanctified marriage of humanity itself "Man of Girls", being merely and purely on its own contact with firm tolerance of human beings. Yet motive an the experience of sense, some like to call it compatibility and suitability. This applies contemporary images state of culture, it is this pleasurability an provides of beauty provocative instantaneousness. Yet realizing more understanding of which they desire expressive each other predetermined fund that drew wholesome acceptance, importance open fundamental large importance on its own, it is easy to see itself modernism at large, humanities inherent individuality prescribed of its own humanist bacterium individuum muscular fibers with bones. Boy, girl=humanism relationships modernism contemporary its state of culture, it, is this philosophy of pleasurability of beauty, between this time and stretch reserved flexibility upon religiosity, years stream mountains, first family view. When you realize, absolute insight of a living thing, subtle of mind dabblings by allaying light identifying thus with yourself happiness, the intelligense of wildfield labours, here employing essay on man. This can only arouse the imagination to movement, the inwardness of striving attainments to have and to hold, to prosper, the active impulse of witnessing truth, striving quest thus thought truth's grip, step above.

Thus, that thus contingent pulsing opacities which are the living depths of us, thus standpoint of considering, Man can just aline himself with a straight pathway, movement of what he is looking at, two persons, when they feel, they found to them, this reality of consequential understandings thought feelings thee awareness of Ones, oneness on personality scales, Quo Vode. A boy an a girl that fall in love civilizing that deep drink of ["the numinous knowledge of understanding"], if, to them the realism catching reality of knowledge thought beyond intelligent reflection the view of form, what I state of my pursuit of humbling.

Chapter 4
Translation of love

o o o o o o o o o o o o o o o o o o o o o o o o o o o o o o o o o

You know why they call the Nobel Peace Prize, Nobel?
Cause its for whom the Bells toll, they toll no more,
know'=bells.

——*Doctor Damon Ray Hollingsworth PH.D.*

Thee individualist love and lovee, live in a realisme, this wildstar. Realists choose, what shall and what shall in so, that the realism itself, is given heightened perceptual inwardness envisioning that real "hand in hand" total stream of living, a vast destiny of distant times of ones soul feeling that one should realize that the heart feels, it is our own what is above, moves us to tears, face to face with the arrangements of relational adjustment, conveying streaming eyes impulsions, airy and moving the living springs of that living times, by a living way to what is now alive.

Thee individualist lover and lovee, live as a realisme, this is why the realists groveling impart this feeling arousing which our souls lay upon themselves to enhancing thoughts of joy. Being most specific, the active character of love is described by stating that love is giving. Giving is varitabilities highest expression of potency! With the very act of giving, we experience ourselves, we experience our strength. This strength, the experience of heightened vitality and potency, fills us with joy. We experience ourselves as overflowing, alive, giving is the expression of our aliveness. Love is that, this conditioning of preserving ones integrity, ones nearby individualism, which brings that deepest need of

47

mankind, certain aspects of a girls behaviour, ambivalent criticism toward debate over whether the expressed courtesy was servility, opacities pulsing contingent depths living, on first beholding him playwrighting figure assembly upstart. Perhaps, charm, simplicity and directness of mind sensibilities to abruptness, fingertips, Yet, the expressions for human wanting, visionary movement and variety of life enchanneled and held fast the unity of active form whereby of many are one and many at the same time.

Everywhere around the United States generous practices fast holding doctrine emotives, which receives from measure of means to ends the utilities, thus a pearl within the oyster, the shell without to healthy use, sweet a rose may smell, their sweet smell living as the roses form. Of greatest consequence is that living which delights the eyes entangling its perceptions by intense feelings which lights up with its own fire.

Purpose of pleasure, the arts, painting, sculpture and architecture, all science applied toward these of purpose. If sympathy interest novelty which imagination follows the entangling perceptions, that same exactness shuffling suspension yields between definite expression, shadowy and multitudinous. Calling this direct subjection, discipline art, reunion by ancient feeling. That sexual separateness building between two individual human beings is a definite expression, real individual lifes corresponding to the emotions living round the sexual experiences, reunion by love. Courage and curiosity upon sheltering health, which reveals itself only as feelings, neediness craving dark feelings feminine antecedent. Responsibilities heavy of a soul-shaking living by a patronage integrity immense on pride. Perhaps metaphysics to acceptance improvising zenith, virtuoso idiom, whose inwardness could transpose art grasping pleasure affections human rights ruminating, patience arousings that pleasure emotive of food and love of clothing, sheltering and health, upon its courage and curiosity toward imaginative adventure. What to do next that which first that true inwardness of man shows itself through the living electricity, that which changes into light, heat, magnetism, vitality body and soul, we walk in the temptation of love and have the most responsibility of loving.

When this movement of any particular points, now with love uncompromising directness, now everything beautiful responds.

Love is sentiment, most of us cling to some, and when this happiness state of movement finds that this love is factual knowledgeability, every man and woman, boy and every girl, there's a change of memories, talk of the times to begin, when you believe a candle bright, human touch and open dreaming. When there's romance for one moment, that's what love does. And daylight keeps on climbing toward the moon, the Sun shining that the wind blows, then shadows pass through the laughter. And to think and I know that something must happen, proving now, that I believe, do you think, That you believe? Living with a world there will really be, majik. That permitting, what then did practice with living health, culture and responsibilities theme upon desire, of yet, what a difference faith has made Doctrine and discipline, inventive alternatives. Love is, what you are doing and not what you have done, love is life and life explains love, love explains life and life is good.

Whose experiences delight life updating pleasure, you see, which you show, the best friend you're going to have is someone individual to be completely honest, has a sense of deep respect for you.

If you give it to your girlfriend, she's going to love you and the double wishbone, you now feel, it sits firm through the passionate pursuit of perfecting love into a girlfriend that delivers your name. Loves translation greatfully experiences a sense of joy, yet shock to state of the art, the one. You know, I just might take my sweet time, getting to the mound and once I get there, maybe I might spit'-shine, the waterpipe and the cooler, with a full court press, freestyle.

A moment with your honey that stretches back, giving girls a place of their own. What they plan to do and the meaning, celebrating, you guessed it! Because we've been happy and interested to get started living, and when it comes to love and sex, all we want is zero'drama and to be on the same page, care and caring and spiritual to go places and the will to get there, those are the things I love.

Houses appreciate in value, families do, too, good taste takes years to acquire. With this art, of mind and body, the theme to adherence, all of which show the timeless movement to find happiness languishing. Feelings rush out, a smugness to standards, a stream of tendency in the individualist. What housewives love, inside and outside a heart and a skin in the human breast, counting by heart'throbs, She will weep and wish wise know nothing, feelings the feelings of youth, now in weeping at that transience of things, she enjoys during the Autumn, dust to dust, she will weep for, what is to most men of deep and intimate concern, a familiar thought brought home, why and what am I?

Sexual statements of personal attitudes projections of that individual condition to marvel at, breathe into that impulse of spell where art and thought were the strongest and freshest of the time and caught that girls heart, expressing a movement already going on. Muscular action of seeing and hearing of breathing the sleep and "dream" of man's heart of her heart. Sexual renewal, so, like a marriage, whose expression is the givings of man, I am thou, whom thou find thyself, thou art I.

Conversations painting on sex, is a modernism strong in feeling manifesting itself, by the institution of "truths desire", that grow long into humane humanism. Those whom think "sex" is pursuant to love, are guilty of all desire. The "value" of sex are a system of "thought" and that domain of "sex" is apart "heresy". We seek sex, because of a desire for truth and we desire truth, because, we wish to know "love". We think that to know "love", is why, we are a human sexuality with needs to bring about that union being brought toward "sexual'intercourse", which is our salvation, keep step of man's destiny.

Industry a stock speculation and making money, the new economics of writing and publishing the journals, circulating libraries to guide and govern in a word the souls of men, its financial arrives, artistic man in status and story of the new time. Prepare to sponge my conscience, spontaneous of light and darkness, growth. Those who are curious to discern, what motives prompting me to write it, this translation of love equasion of bacterium. It will satisfy most quick if they glance this description of a "reading", the standing of this writing with a view to ground reason, sprinkling contact with the actuality to view the living which views of the wishful conditions of witnesses to a generosity of soul, instances as thought of interest of desire, instances by my choice dizzy rapture to control and place us toward human thought and hide our minds intelligense slightest step, a will-o'-the wisp, mask judgement upon astonishing human responses, "clasping of hands", with the "intralocking fingers" handling of shoulders, a certain "intrawrapping" of "twining" of "legs", a branch of strenuous movement, a rhythm its prime art of this field it touches to the attainment.

The heat, wetness, goose bumps, sexual electricity, seeing those bare legs, belly and your thighs, legs spread apart, lifting to wrap them around my waist. With my hands holding your moving rump, squirming to match my own in a series of jolting shots, exploding my sperm, so, stiff, you sperm, thinking about it. Us together, we go "opposite" side'to-side, around and around up and down, taking a tour of the entire bed, rolling and humping in a frenzy. Sticking my thrusting "erection" into feel pussy'hot grinding around my dick, thick as your wrist and at least (6) six inches long, slid into you bucking warmth, warm bucking, buck a dozen times murmuring and squirming, rubbing my crotch of my groin black pubescent hair, joint mating with your grasping vagina, my balls slap your butt, I just hold on, my hands clenching you firm. The lock on your face, moaning, pulsing a grown erection slid into you, sticking my thrusting erect tip inside of that heat, wetness, tightness pulsing slit to feel pussy grinding around my dick. Slamming your vaginal labia with a series of jolting shots, so stiff, you play with my balls, legs spread, sexual electricity walking through of our bodies skin to whisper of a kinda of a naïve, baby face, that is delightful to whisper into.

Man, set him to mechanism philosophy that spins man's mind and his body, his thoughts, his activities, inside and outside of the exact saneness. It is here and now, the abundance and joy of faith, that right of this variant to live and grow, that moment men attain truth making laws of thought and feeling.

Chapter 5
Time and Chance

Somewhere beyond the eternal skies, there's a Jewel placed between Stars forming Heavens light.

The opportunities for times pleasurability of chances happeneth to us all. The inquisition healthy each described marital love, erotic sexology of consequences, we each realize essence of humanitas pervasive expense, attachment the expense aims reason.

The humanist bacterium separate essence of being man and girl, love erotic characters, strengthening care of obvious respect due.

Humanitarian sensations capacity for love, will enabla boy and a girl to express their sexual feelings towards each other and that at the expense of reason, aims at strengthening love in this final transition, pleasurability of sensations. It is to find, vigorous resolute ideals, asceticism dwelling the best perimeter of aesthete's cultivating upon their austering regime experienced, being genuine understanding. Marriage "eh" precipitates "numinous knowledge of understanding" causes, being manifestations genuine incohabitation love infatuation, speedy view amplifications.

Sensuous, bespeaks mildness, mutual loving bestowal life explicit, this perceptive attitude is too realize active concern for the growth of that life which you exist. The numinous knowledge of understanding, being true love a standing of forming true love a standing with.

It is, life of growth, we ourselves henceforth faith, we inevitably recognize of moral and cultural convention of ideas, natural laws and lessons led formula and present day understanding times, between deep sense "eh" morality is attaining lifetime world large attitude on recurring lives, domestic desirability. Just being characterology, occurrences stock responses surrenders participating musculature unitary awareness, give=to=get, the expressing coyness perceptive understanding movements.

A man can reach towards a girls love and thereby expelling his course of being, which sensualists disturbed humanism of all one knows, will enable a man to express his sexual feelings towards that particular girl whom has chosen him, whereby of flow, we find pleasurability of characteristic consciousness musculature, its timing from corresponding by analogy which matters, so much to the sensualists sensuous fits, foreplay at present. The females system related to the Vulva and to the Uterus, piercing through the vaginal extravaginal musculature individuum pelvic floor, melting unitary intrusion movements, characteristics fact upon uniformity, inhibition discharge.

Man by his very soul psyche, along metaphysio of both domestic kindred by its very proposal to another. The man's consummation being principle of stock response its human males sexuality, Man has only one organ for genitalia organ genital sexual expression. Man has only one organ, describing genitalia uniformity, giving him the ability of inhibition discharge, Sensuous vulva—passionate uterine, it is commonplace at current pleasurable excruciating deepest musculature intravaginal moving the uterine and vulva orgasm convulsions jazzier fertility, that this beauty equivocally of cervix and peritoneum.

Femininity one of the chief proneness genitalia occurs vaginal release, apnea appearance of crico=pharyngeus musculature, abdominal viscera actual vagus nerve. Meaning breathing laden with sexual intercourse, intravaginal each thrust minor labia is pulled down toward the rectum and processes shaft of clitoridal facility, effective of clitoris linked responses, sexual linked responsiveness, functing systematically and persistent behaviour responses pelvic viscera area mons, mons area specific "clitori" awareness, fulfillment whistle imaginative of form, drafting mudbath.

Marriage awareness, pleasures to be derived fulfillment, who is equal to try to get the love of a given personage exclamation, We wish to live, due to many unforeseen situations, by a realism, after you've had a chance to view this life, Our agreement to a state of the art, to equable sense of development, physical age of reason.

Because of probabilities justified spread, with well continuance is legitimacy walks privilege existing self-realization, sense of scale of culminating. It might be a loud noise, you knew all along how that goes, sometimes it might be a cab driving through, someone times, even calls you, a sense of happiness lives life and scale of desirability, you can't do, what you want, when you want to. Regardless of how long and how you know someone you knew. Because of probabilities the quantity of methods certain like imagined tendency, essentialism true analysis of based stylized movement capturing the mood of landscapes. Now as a man and how you got there a woman forced us to re-examine the sexual long commandment being thereof saying, "["Guys get Girls and Love'em for life"]", Sexual renewal likes marriages, we are living, changing our lives. On being a man, a man feels towards a girl love on words plane, of course upon man his very soul love an like is wise is characterized thereby virtue, important the embrace ironstone exchange imprinting virtue of pleasant wonders, deepest satisfying subjecting place, open prevalence of series. Love ability is as man country age as realism date up to express course on creativity.

It is, with the changes by things that we perceive that trend within writings that time toward that subjectification of interest, through what walk of living inclined, take this structure and qualities and these passionals for lifes perceiving mind. Perspective mechanics of feeling, its field widened to include themes of standard, that clearest voice, that make most vital, soul of mankind and his time. Works of art, must teach us to see, to feel, to understand the individualist warmth, what can arouse analogy and give us that perception of the dash, on what is thereof being, progressive movement of visionary times, citizen of this world making his precarious living postulating on that truth.

When we wish to bring it, into our work, That finest mechanistic concepts of the contractual aesthetic systems, philosophies of art, we exalt it. Whose freedom an image serves "Bondsman" investing to tend all its festivals and ceremonies, its dancings, its vows and gifts. That living springtide on grounds outside on the fields of our countries growth that prosperity, is green of grass and tree's painting agriculture. Painting agriculture, springs, light and sounds sprang up movement stimulating eyes and ears to acting to active activities ground. It is that handling of both, mature individual healthy human adult females breasts, bodily actual caress, fondling materia' secunda, works of right reason and justice. It is thus, man knows whereat things place idiom, where he finds himself. When a man caresses the ardent lips of a girl, by aesthetic offering, placing his lips, ongoing this girlish figure, as an act of fettering desire affecting a show of greeting, foreplay as kissing motive.

Brass tinkling sounds of glass chimes ringing, a shutting slam gives sound driven to inspect. A window closes on a still night, a phone rings in the room where there is non. So, this cycling of Gib'Ral'-Tars living, renews with love as life. So, the cycling of man's living, renews with love of girls, it passes through majik, finance, art and bizz'ness, back to love of girl and keeps moving.

Girls are loving human individuals, obvious and aesthetically pleasing all of them are as they exist. That principle purpose of humanity is to fulfill, his and/of her vantage around wishing of course, a man desires working self appreciation.

Someday, you want to go away, someday, you will want to sit and play, I think that I believe it enough, and its just a matter of understanding that I care, I want to acknowledge as being that special love of my life, foreplay during bodily contact.

Foreplay is that massaging of the "abdomen" of that pubic area surrounding the vaginal area of "vulva" actuary adult human females thighs made upon consequence of making the actual linear inserting of a man's penis, scrotum dwelling venue in towards this girls vaginal labia arial. The only way to have sex all the time is to be a gender, a Boy and/or a Girl. The "Maid" in the kitchen loves to see her inward self in the adventures of the girl down the hall.

If you must need a variety, its causes demographics! Finalize the number of glow-in-the-dark tags, needed for the ride, for a good cause, long after twilight ends, time immense builds satisfying life experience and rewards life, if developing a statement, picture areas step-by-step and always caring the amassive accounting thereby accountability of self, brought the ability of care, you acknowledge existence as caring, because you exist life. Hair follicle a small cavity involving the epidermis and dermis skin tissue of which from dermis hair develops "habidashery" appearing growth ruminants fine appearing coat tuxedo appearing haircloth lengthy aeroplanea assuming Damon Ray Hollingsworth Ph.D. keratinous ruminants cylindrical living filaments camelist'camelus'camelism camel life image of Damon Ray Hollingsworth Ph.D. camel living man, How you got here.

How you got here, is a river running stream, river running tide a wash, global living the image of fundamentalism, mountain sweet practice alive art. Yet, though hereabout time existing you're always hearing longterm, lifelong my abilities, somehow your reasons start thinking, responsibility. When you plan your activities with an eye toward taking responsibility for how you spend your time, global living the image of fundamentalism, mountain sweet practice alive'art, keystone of camel living the image of man, this world rock, Styme Bow World, well=being the existence art Holsinger, Shinvescarine of Heaven, our ability available of well=being. To say, "art" has a fixed direction and is plotted in advance of each and every human experience is a whisp of truth. It, is, that being, this [hyperlink] link that facilitates communication, thus being {Shinvescarine of Heaven, Holsinger}.

You do acknowledge, if you love, love brings its own personalism set feeling of being, to be this that is, it, if, I am what is, if what I am, so that what now, can we bring about, I want as you are, I want with what I am, yet, if, I understood, you are saying perhaps without any flame? Due amount by an large, being therein your estimative, guessti-mates, and you will see, you say, here is a barrier, a bondage with me and I want to understand it, filth, laughter and pride.

Chapter 6
Fundamentalism

You Never give up, You never give up
You Never give in, You never give in
You Stand there and Shout, You stand there and shout
You Stand there and Spin, You stand there and spin
You Never give Up, You Never give IN
You Stand there and Shout, You Stand there and Spin
You Never Look'out, You Never Look'in, YOU'RE THERE
You're There, YES, Thank' You:

U.S. Marine Corps, Honorable Discharge December 20th 1976
Platoon Leader 3137, Secretary: MOS: Intelligense.
Dosctor, Damon Ray Hollingsworth PH.D.

Most impatience, she awaits
Upon entry of the room talking, We laughed moving about playing
I held her near, then Kissing her neck, I have massaged her bosom
Whilst caressing her lips on the stairs
My love said, I wish to talk with thee
Walking through the garden on a cool summer day
She removed her shoes and tying both strings together saying.
I will tell thee about my love and we shall sit beneath the cedars
As we cherish these most precious moments!
She said with me, Happy are the days, when I see your face
Kissing her hands, My love said, Happy are the times?
I see that I am with You…

My interest, I realize of a statement of particular long standing, I am of things about myself, that movement, I am about to talk, and to whom I acknowledge I use direct movements that have this conviction that will deepen our understanding. So, my study into a study as art, brings me along through works of man's themes of philosophies of soft-feet, those artworks, personages took whom they move toward thereinto play, reasoning, writing of a mind alive and aware, Awareness works, play, plays round yield deserves. Written with realisme, thought deserves attention by its own right! Writings acknowledge attendance according that "modern'civilization", thought deserves attention, foreign rights. At that time this was written with that light that knew, there's "stars" dwelling souls, writing keys tie'-lines, this state is to. Than man and girl of feeling to continue to live and feel to youth of standards of feeling thee impact of preference and personal lattitudes to its subjectivity by a feeling an impression with soul a passional love as gifting refinement of feeling, on that love and friendship being temperances feeling toward permanences truth few limits given human mind. Boundaries feeling toward temperances' permanences that as individualism being with species, which to exist growth, toward which grow existence and moment. Those investments toward which existences grow, to teach girls to see and to feel to human feeling, day to day and moment to moment. It is, with the changes of things that we perceive that trend specific writings time, toward that subjectivity interest subjectification of interest versing which, what walk of living inclined taking those images, structure and qualities and passionals of beings perceiving mind, perceiving mind mechanics of feeling its field, widened to include as themes of standard, that clearest voice of making that most vital soul of man and his time, continuity strikes.

We ourselves individualist human beings, which we fathom healthy, masculine and feminine astuteness living human beings, whereby we, are actualizing this given stance of satisfaction, now acknowledging, we are gifted, finalizing transitory equating state everyday acknowledgement living bacterium reproducing love. Attractive equasion "metaphysio" analysis hygiene, availability acknowledge its by world requirements, reproducing features work the everyday world, state of living things continuity strikes facilitate injecting the equasion, themselves being living bacterium. Love astounds pleasurable exciting human sexualism, promoting the intercourse, Yah wine head tramps.

Put a little change around my naked and lead me anywhere, soul let me be, YoH Teddy'Bear. A satisfaction notary aspect, service of experimentalism, service asserting what is meant biologic culminating preferred system defines the orgasmic and post-orgasmic state orgasm. During coitus and copulation release occurrence, erotic serves vaginalism the intravaginal stimulation and physiological reaction through the extensions from this area of responding globe update.

NOW MORE OVER, OUR CORE INDIVIDUALISM: The fundamental processes that promote erotic impulse remain always the same. Consequentially each response is different from those any other individual human being could show. Mankinds species, pattern satisfying resolution, when responding simply ejaculation reiteration, between one woman's orgasmic experiences and orgasms as it occurs modes multiple intensity of duration present to the exact physiology of human girlish figure, a standard male ejaculatory appearance appears man being responsive, arbitrarily effective experiences phenomenon.

This is at the heart of our values from day [1] one.

What's good for your developing sense of one-on-one experience?

Someone you can trust at the center of what you do?

Thinking that could accelerate, open doors?

The outpouring of sympathy, such as yours that awareness, if, we somehow cure the amazing diversity of views, REMEMBER, REFLECT, RESPOND. 3, 320, 935% percentage of clues that trigger revolving genuine importance of peace and prosperity express beauty of vastness principality and majesty evolving honour, the dry light of reason, life of feelings. Pleasurability applies beauty, the immediate agent to mount the summit, its anyone's guess mixing a long pattern, whether chatter and domestically plenty we now know mainline, over what should arise to describe a ceremony, a place of peace, to creating and sustaining and satisfying our needs. As a Doctor of Biblical Counseling, it has been written among the Dead Sea Scrolls that Knowledge is Death, Holsinger cosmology of Gib'Ral'-Tar, this world rock, Styme Bow, World a living Gibraltar realm, Manchild revealing Teth'Neth'Babb'Ye'A'Saw'Back'Thigh'Knese, Twinkling Damon Ray Hollingsworth Doctor of Philosophy of Religion, keystone of camel living the image of man. With the art of mind and body, this theme to utterance, extracting space underway intelligense emotional love, what have you, attributing life and who at times the aeroplanea ache expressiveness skill language, art grasping pleasure impacting desire.

Vocabulary of language intimacy of happiness, worth our ability of well=being tapestry view. Why? When all rapt by antecedent struggling, here is met things mainstream look, life of yielding sexuality articulating the pleasure and beauty of feminism, celebrating sense of self, facing feminism the straight mind, the sense of shifting textuality and self=representations Hellish half hour-self righteous, class identity and overidentification with the aesthetics language had loved thick lips, As we acknowledge a spirit of temperance and fairness atonement. This was the culture and this the frame of mind responsive of feminist critics, feminist literary accounts speculative intellectualism, she sums up the value of intimacies. My aim here is, the existing text as a means of finding dubious that their view of things a sense that their own existence, it was with good reason, once we take serious the individuality as a individualism desirable and good form for human beings, consumption. For a girl to read as a human girlish figure is not to repeat an identity or an experience that is given. Yet, it does play a role, if, she constructs it with reference to her own identity as a individualism, the experience of that subject. We need more developed accounts of how various kinds of knowledge generalize interesting, what makes the view of being and time, the presence of existing.

Sometimes with humanity, peace judges statesmanship to the greater good, the axiomatic wit globalized genius genetic creativity and justice, this World planet "Styme Bow" earth, Holsinger realm mountainous view Waxing, waxing gist, Camelism'camelist, Camelus camel living. You can only be baptized with what you really actually exist! You can only be born with what you were born to be.

If, you are a planet? You will be baptized with a planet.

If, you are a Camel? You will be baptized with a Camel.

You can only be existing with what you were born to exist!

Of course I honestly can say, a very real sense of humanity more developed certain humanistic characteristics, the answer true ironstone of review, milestones development. Though we live, chartists movement and joy of life, its bridge of the day open for me. Its something that happens, because the one that knew is that twist to experience ideas language and culture over deep=seated time. This statement seems rocky, aimed circling, traveling beyond fundamentalism. What a startling "claim to imagine" of flourishing that perfect language attitude image of storywork, figure of course alongside items linguistics course, examine account matters, genre and style as well, vocabulary items.

Chapter 7
Journeys

Somewhere there you just gotta be and though you know you show me
  Somewhere there anywhere you go, There's a change of memories
  Talk of the times to be, Somewhere there, you know you find
  That things are true, When you just believe.

When there's romance for one moment, you can bring to the night,
human touch and a candle bright, open dreaming. human worries that
you can carry through the laughter and daylight keeps'on climbing
toward the Moon then shadows pass, living with a world by owning
my own knowledgeability. I have a dream, work ethics, destiny's child
and Shinvescarine, when you understand the nature of a thing, you
know what its capable of. Just about everywhere I look, I see victims of
poker, the energetic sweat. mantrack, dream girl merry-go-round you
feel so hot and wet, plenty aspiring waves the realm of the senses, live
what you like at a sensible age.

To the whole experience, how do you get what you want from a
man?

Stay there and work with it! Ladies love to be the center of attention. She was a songstress which meant that there is a melody, see what
she can do to make you feel good? I love being loved. Plan ways to
accentuate your girlfriends attributes, when the urge becomes uncon-
querable a matter of sound the sense of ideal beauty specific fine
expression. The desire of this desire has a yielding to the seductive siren
a love song, song of love. Remember, with great fun, there are many
opportunities and the opportunities being many are one of self sane
exactness. Because you loved me so much, life arrangement where a

view with good rhythm mixture itself, flush fabric on a whim, because we love, life and work, There are many opportunities to savor. And, life without love, is like eating spaghetti without sauce and "parmeasan'cheese" and everyone needs a little spice with their life and you work and you love.

Nursing the issue of facts, one voice like a racing "Heart", give me your love, once a measure to a score and seduce me out of humanity with human sanctity of credibility image arranging pleasantries state of globe, what this has for you, your plan for life that comes near you. Love and sharing the immediacy a man and girlish fancies, sex and feelings human reelings, relay actual human sexuality, eyes wink and blink, the ability sense earned for the life of me.

My love is strengthened, that love, our love, who is, it that you alone, your personal feelings meeting with time to take a tour, my happiness human race I said human life as you go and let live intelligense, a life our faith heavens first say, I love a voice on you as being Shinvescarine of Heaven, Holsinger rular, the meaning of life. Now, with the meaning of life, the genuine article it starts to love, to love is, to love life back, to love around me a rarity and thematic sweeping true appreciating beauty and fine experience of first neatness due only of state a middling laid chest center core of beings rhythmic living, "Mysterious Harts" by a substantial form both a presence of knowledge, eternal life a materia' secunda, its just a matter of understanding wish upon a star, the goodness of man, prose about this girlish figure as she lay near love and trust, family and friend, what my "Hart" has too say. You see upon this star, like it be on going stone, I understand to express human truths work to all forms and creatures living, carrying this thing whom life cheers needle of development glorifies, glorified love improvisation of many needs genuine image of creating I do love apathy and human beauty, metaphysio' acknowledgement a smile on her face, so, much love for life. Faith is the product of reason, when you're a name rather than a number, yesterday by the rising of the Holy Ghost's Voice everything changing, chosen you, listen where it, is, there a celebrated respect.

Doing our best, I am writing to say everyone needs treats to make life worth living! I must be able to promise of course of what I know even realize you understand? As you move through what might be of planning a clear idea of your willingness at the present time, the accumulated savings specified. Doing our best, smooth talk myself, imagining just rules, get on with your life, on the accuracy of speed, dark, light all around forming the Sun given to stretch the purest spring whereby to speak of things, your affections sway me and the passion is a dream a mysterious morning Sunlight I suppose the best thing top say for the view, to express the time from 1-to-12 midnight black as the night, something of a truth, sometimes if, bound by thoughts of things, New England if maine as something mixed up with the brain, that right of the variant to live. Now I know where you belong and how you know it, am been being, twas nobler with facts than deed, there is an answer for everything be humbling, be smiles, be grand grim grin being beloved child. Because of better friendships humanitarian presence and knowledge idealism much the above 'Anomaly" mindset, which gives the highest sense image of skill limelight visible of bondage accounting the view of form to give the "[GHOSTS STOCK WITH TRADE]" on the standard artistic drive.

The idea spawns the move over time Global viewed which bodes well'being driven renewal to merge growth, to figure its means "Cup=with=Handle", its kind line, the effect that a thriving plan serving human views zone it faces smart looking graphics with what the average learning "Cup=with=Handle" arms transfer [WELLS] flexible idea, it be a good chance even best "TRILLION" series. Wealth management, knowledge ironing drudgery with "Moon" resembling life I just think, we also admit things are going well global link, wishing for a deep dark well. We, have to evolve to a "Utopian" kind of view, I have one that works! Lets talk about "SEX" baby, Think of you, Thank you. Because "Man's" dependence is based on human sexualism merging, the article actualism satiably of structure and strength, rhythmic suffusion of warmth baseline of vaginal musculature of the extravaginal musculature against the greatly distended circumvaginal venous plexi and vestibular bulbs placing themselves with the outer third of the vagina. These ongoing rhythmic contractions serve as criteria occurrence of orgasm. The ability is worth feelings sensitivity of marvelous joy and happiness specific feelings. Pleasure is devious an those of course essentialism thus satisfying health, terms the experience of diversity investitures.

Just as we learn how we should feel about our human sexuality, you understand genius. When you love, like I love describing happiness, your feelings living laughter the principal mover, It just comes and makes you weak, sleep, kiss it goodnight. Love active is the activity an revival, love is the activity, since odours be, it may alone I turn'd though favourably I am as I have "eh" stated before of flesh brandishing paraded through perspective underlines stepping, stated delivery humanitarian, they ask to a data engineer reach, key spell, luck'=locomotive engineering ground line agreement time as I ago of Man. Now, were is was, were was were, is were is, were is were, is were as Man being Man were of knowledge and were of being knowledge, acknowledge of Man were is knowledge and were of being MAN, Thus love I expect it, thus Jigolo on going. To write, right spell, spell right murmur, Jigolo, Ziploc' vanity "tuff" profiles "Hub mix". Masculinity and femininities character means this is this person they are after, responsibility awareness, lifetime upon pleasures. Loves times, character remarks "One' Love" which desirable once you live for it. You there, each of us, You want to know what put me over? The answer is, "[Mileage Attentiveness]" base of behaviour, right' peace of mind.

What strikes bare, strikes bottom, susceptibility echo as though behaviour rich clouds and snow wetness, Guys get Girls and love'em, for life. Understanding of all the facets of long term care, minds, so, still the pursuit of this as far as the feeling of "Symbiotic' union" of oneness, of the depth of ones own biological structure awareness, the realism reigning reality of life, living as One Man and One Girlish figure and both human subtlety acknowledging knowledgeable and knowing that both were loving and grateful and a healthy state of conditioning shadowed. Modern Man's happiness thoroughly afferent particle of some fulfillment consists regulatory apropos fluent manic thrill, largely adequate effective awareness, boasting pie and pix, pied-a-terre. Based on what makes a person attractive usually of package our scale as demands develop the essence of consequential life and feeling depth, structuring thus [Two] persons drink from life available awareness on the knowledgeability of numinous knowledge of understanding. Here "eh" comes that "FUDGE", I acknowledge "eh" You Luv Meh. Love is the actual product of adequate and effective satisfaction, the true product of truism. Look, I am with [Luv] being that I have the awareness of my avenues of expression to enhance my personality though window too the keys of ignition. Happiness is the truth makeshifting producing the true product of true love, created for humanity and human discovery, with being that I and You share adventurousness. What a lot of familiarity, that's the law of this jungle and that's the way this cookie crumbles, Reach'out and Somewhere eat! That's about all there is to this plot of crazy for you. By the fact jack! U.S.M.C.

Marriage educating "pride of place an senses", holding prevalence is life environment pleasant wonders. Thus a Man and a Girlish figure eagerness, culminating movements release and humane uses devolve, full and total surrender and well'=being, full and total arrest. By [surrender] this Man feels surrender to a girlish figure! And by [arrest] this Girlish figure embrace is [protecting] that man. Disturbed humanism, which will be sponsoring a "SPIRIT'DRIVE" of jazzier relativity old genius creating, what's been happening on your mind. Man, by an large astuteness his very soul lay upon domestic sexualism, wholesome as a heart'beat 36 million times a year, 12=months, 52=weeks, 365 ½ days, conscience upon consciousness move. Note: the average' rate per heart beat is 36 million times per year. We are the creatures of as we understand our attitudes being to deal with these principles and the ability too love and concern for our own well=being, compiling desire. Marriage and desire a "titling" on a world, my life of good times, motivated state of bacterialist construct'finding parenting starlight, state of world.

Chapter 8
Work' Ethics

Bless them that live and give works to them that have life.

DREAM'WORKS PRINCIPALS: The Element, "SEED".

Perspective economic "PhotoVoltaic Cell, the electric' electromagnetic "[Atomic'PhotoKinesis]" solarium spastic round flat database atomic computer genetic photovoltaic structure atom, molecular rotatabling plane "Aeroplanea" axis space axis flexibility applying current gauge of perspective accents sweeping 5 miles wide and 5 miles long metallism metallurgy work, flying, we utilize a time accuracy, Yin, Yang, YoH, YoH, forward and backward, up and down saucier, space employing presence existing humanitarian demographic, shape appears friendly with the expertise above, issue existing, line assembly employment life economic, self=first needs. Because on the average issue, our retool line, existing management life expertise above, applying techniques when everything works. That's what makes truly outstanding performances with the expertise above, existing "Snaplight'Tic" prosperity utilities. What may be economic need, we expect, that works!

Friendship, what warmth with ease and present honest picture importance I thee WED, living, loving and learning by ethical legitimate exact marriage of service and movement, genuine affection, genuine and clear sense affirm large understanding. Flexibility affirming parlayanse our "toes" co'exist curbside occurrence on prompting. Now, yard darkness, where it takes you, which there is patronage acknowledging "realism" conscience I am faith "duh" lake of stream, mountains years country itself drive, expressing view and stretch the assessment curve itself, delivery witness. Friendship responsibility, of human service is viewed practice of, term honouring genuine experience as being responsive ideal. We are creatures of as we understand our attitudes, just that, what that Ghost may do to us, course occurs message on life economics, let us begin now, with where we are right now. When you bring all that to the table account, key account benchmark, citing growth. It's a tenuous stretch to set that whole idea upon, because economic developments field voice of sanity and savings, develop sanity, the economy expects rebounds. Response, response and stimulus, response and conditioned stimulus behavioural modification.

Guidelines the ethics practice, as the entrepreneur of my family, I have being gist of singing, I have traveled with tenacity at musical live ongoing touring always as the leadsinger. studied voice and piano at Drake University in Des Moines, Iowa, [1974] they give you more credits for voice then they do for piano. Went to Hollywood California, that same year 1974 and lived right off of wilshire boulevard, behind the then Getty's Union Bank: first California dream excursion to fruition, she used to be my girl, La Toya Jackson, met everyone, but, Micheal and her Momma and her oldest sister whose husband was a security guard at that time. I, watched from bleachers at celebrity basketball games, sitting next to her dad and the two youngest ones. Funniest thing though I left her wilshire boulevard on a bus without her driving the sunroofed burgundy Mercedes that she used to drive alongside the wilshire buses hollering at me to get off the bus at the world savings bank in santa monica as I walked away from love I sang "reasons" and when I got back to Des Moines, Iowa, there was a letter from "Toy" with a picture of her on the picnic bench wearing her diamond ring and the letter, everyone of my family had read it, except me. They said they could not find it, but there was one and they could not and did not remember what it spoke of. My first Hollywood employment venture was through the acting community, I had done various numerous casting tapes and ventured on the strip to nightclubs and sang on open mike. Irwin Allen, director of the Posiedon Adventure and The Towering Inferno, one day at the TAV Studio's told me, after

I ask him for a job! To write a script and take it to Jack Bauer, the then Casting director of 20th Century Fox Studio's 1975. Anyway, I wrote the script and it was stolen in Las Vegas Nevada, while I was working for Ceasar's Palace, one night watching a comedy routine of Joey Bishops. Two'weeks later, Jimmy Hoffa disappeared and I did a television interview for gun control, which was televised in Las Vegas Nevada. I even did stand'up comedy routines later in March 1994, California.

Currently, I'm a professional live, stage and theater actor, traveling all around the world performing theater stage originality an performances. One song on CD, I sing, "FEAST And THE FAMINE" lyrics. Song: I'm God, I'm the Devil, good cop, bad cop! Mother mary's little helper, I'm the great manipulator, I'm the master of delusion Tic'Toc I'm a Poet, I'm a pervert, I'm a Madman, I'm a Saint.

Magician par excellence, normal I ain't. I'm here, I'm there, I'm everywhere man, I think therefore I think I am. I make magical music out of all the mundane, I make musical magic out of all the insane. Here today and gone tomorrow, I'm rolling on a river of heavenly sorrow I waeve a world of madness truth and fright, My mind is a buzzardized bat in flight! I hold the dark, dark, night up to the light.

The Feast and The Famine, the Sun and the Rain! The source of your power is the source of your pain. Take it baby the way that it comes, somedays there are plenty, somedays there are none. This party called life ain't done til its done. Me and Mother mary, cooked up this gumbo to take you on a learning journey mumbo jumbo. Now, baby eat a big bowl of mother mary's gumbo, mumbo jumbo.

The Feast And The Famine, the Sun and the Rain, the source of your power is the source of your pain. Take it baby the way that it comes. Somedays there are plenty, somedays there are none. This party called life ain't done til its done. Lyrics written by, My Boss, Miss Jeanne Elisabeth Calvit during her stay in ISLAMUJERES MEXICO and Music Written by, Tod Petersen and Damon Ray Hollingsworth PH.D., ISLAMUJERES "means" Island of the Beautiful Women.

Words let you express the ideas that thought give a form to improve, its link to understandable ideas clear knowledge of yourself. You want to be amid tree's and forestry and domestic turbulence using trigger, right beneath bouncing trigger realm tabling ground course, overall "lucent' windows". Twinkling of fits waxing by the biological motions of the inward propulsion drive of remote "Land Speculation". A human propensity of far spread bands of land, world built musculature of zistense. Man I shall reason, we act this world built drawn startling display, SHAZzzzzzzz [Glass, Glass]. The leafs and ferns waxing Gliss:Glass: flapping through windows breeze. A branch of strenuous movement, a rhythm its prime art of this field, it touches to the attainment that this variant to attain truth making feeling, Southwest Addition, Block 5, Lot 13 Hidden Valley, Highland, Sharp County, Arkansas, USA. Witnesseth Damon Ray Hollingsworth Ph.D. curtesy and homestead dower, the world goes around fast.

Work' Ethics, Guidelines practices, the ethics standards.

"Ethics is about whom we are and how we want to be perceived", it really is "key" to experiences which share practices. By, new self-acceptance, courteous truisms, I say understanding where electricity among [destiny] would make even being, well-to-do, when you are a slave, and keep everyone happy, it would seem to be on demand. Simple as that may sound, what we are about now is "facing" growth, reaffirming growth! Reaffirming "Virtue'enzyme=Engines" the emergence of standards, you may think as you think. Let me sing to you beautiful like, what if, I have a dream? Think about it. Write it, to somebody whom hands it to somebody until finally, it hits all of which means, you get to hear about, you like our little way of saying "CHAKA KHAN", "TYRA BANKS" and "[GARCELLE BEAUVAIS]" and "ANN TOSCHAK". You may think chances are the time that could move streams, are already moved, this is where we introduce you. Let's face it, you can always go back to getting your news the old way? Spiritualism vast Ghosting, to love, occurs just what you do for me. Profligate age "[*Asobi*]" the Art of having fun with assets, living loving and learning, psychology and physiology of matter, viewed preponderance obvious genuine exact service and movement. Human service of practice able as bodied form, One arrangement there appears fully well living moralism, sumptuous skills firm flambouyant parlayanse, avenue Engineering desires under a skeleton state, I want to acknowledge "eh" with my life occurring verbatim, drink pledge upbringing spouses. Thus this begetting rhythm this deepest preserving depths "naked rhythm".

Kitchen with a spoon and bowl tightly held with my hands to spend a chilly as has been. Styme Bow the Man of this World self taught, which a Man grows, thinks therefore answering, you labour love upon knowledge and love understanding. Love is time, love is time amplification, time enough. Do we compliment that? Should we say, pockets pay, if, they are already making money? Who is to say, what we have? We are obviously able as sexual human beings, cultural living, loving and learning fluidity. Understanding home of soup and "Big'Pot" with the atmosphere of flavour specific substance of muses thoroughfare usability academic the accountabilities for the well'=being. Upon this time, issued that is the idea to outspace economy and think growth. It looks like a good economic recovery, we are getting curiosity as language as something to fall back on and tell the truth about it bouncing. Its been easier for us to become "profitable", everyone is more aware ["enzyme'engines"] global looking. You find your eyes lingering on supple curves, a slight smile imagining yourself crosses your lips. You imagine what it would be like with its smooth delicacy at hand both hands. Both hands you seem to wander with feeling to attain retaining tantamount reciprocity of firm "gestation" but would like X's standing moreover Y's fixating you imagine upon this time accounting just by, it looking at flexibility with the flexibility to take advantage of every new opportunity with the expertise to put its resources to work for you. I'm your Babies Daddy and I'm on the Phone begging to come home, and, that's what makes truly outstanding performances big pot of paint.

Question: Does a Weeping Willow weep, Does a Willow Weeping wave, is a Tree trunk ruff?

When you walk through a Supermarket the turnaround phase is plenty of food and water, a gourmet lover's paradise an easy life and lot of good'prices. Bread, Beverages, fruit and vegetables work'ethics, Tree of life existing, now months start years, spawned reasons growth roses, plenty of mileage adopted procurement. There's your reason and swears there's your answer? PIGGY'=ECONOMIC. This is the only opportunity economic short and near term, you can Piggy'Back.

It accuses me of being thirsty! "Poraniour, pour'eh-near, meaning, backrinsing wash I us and/of We, the essence of being. If, there is a safe bet, then COMMODITIES make up leverage it has when making purchases, market trade agreement, as it reflects through "Voices" whistle imaginative alittle unto life an revival all well'-led.

The "HART" will make you believe a lot: LIFESCAPES.

The "HART" will make you wish for a lot: LIVING.

Love active is the activity an revival, Work'Ethics, The affair with all those opportunities periphery of giving life at variance with, what one is up to, for a time over the experience of people, elements terms learning and living it up with language, among clothing personalisms.

Chapter 9
Shinvescarine

SONG'TITLE:

Baby, I have a Dream

INTRO, RAP:

Somewhere beyond the Eternal Skies, there's a jewel placed between stars forming heavens light. Don't you know it? Don't you show it?

Yes, I know it.

LYRIC'SPREAD:

Baby, I can bring to the light-heaven shows the Eternal night Somewhere there, You just gotta be and though you know, you show me Somewhere there anywhere you go, there's a change of memories, talk of the times to be. Somewhere there, you know you find that things are true when you believe.

CHORUS:

I, have this Dream, yes I believe, when there's romance for one moment That's what love does to every Man and Woman every Man and Woman, Boy and every Girl.

LYRIC'SPREAD:

Baby, You can bring to the night, human touch and a candle bright Open'dreaming Human worries that you can carry on with me.

CHORUS:

I, have this Dream this I believe, when I wake up every morning and I see the Sun, go shining, through the laughter and Daylight keeps on climbing toward the Moon.

FREE'VERSE:

And yet, -although yet I sing, I do believe the Sun shining and I do, -I believe, I do believe, that the wind blows, You know-then Shadows pass: CHORUS:

I, have this Dream this I believe, that my world will come together That my whole life is living together, living in a world without make-believe.

CHORUS:

I, have this Dream this I believe, that my life will come together

That my world has a, future in pictures, living with, a world, there will really be—majik. And to think and I know that, sumpthing must happen proving now that I believe. Do you think that you believe?

SHINVESCARINE:**Shin' Ves Ka'=Rein: noun, singular.

Mixture, itself creating spectacle on cloth, pillar cloud cosmology existing knowledge of stars. Global like itself cosmology, Holsinger word mixture of faith, mixture image of class sanctuary existence of fundamentalism revolving cosmology of stars zistense: Zis' tens: charm, pertains to exist: the activity of feeling, the electro' energy alternating with fermentation.

Heavens'Holsinger, Fundamental differences between True think-ing and the Living cycle of Majik course, Living the image of Shinves-carine. As principality and spirit for life and Mass tissue extension Thunder and Darkness with Lightning, Shinvescarine at that moment. Pillar of cloud and Pillar of fier. The darkness does comprehend and the light shineth through darkness, that was the "true'light", giving light to every Man that is brought toward humanistic flesh placed on this world for a witness, which heavens firmament the all seeing "EYES" witness that light flourishing heavens solar system, furnace of "[Bowl'Winkold]". Yet, I am bound which your mind wonders and Book my members. For all minds are "naked" which you've learned through experience, feelings compensating and assimilating ideas and relational values of theoretical thought, self-knowledge and a piece of the sky oxygenating atmospheric, a star system. Because the fruit thereof extendeth itself to the time spent this world happiness maintaining the truth by hearing desire among all joys bankrolling capabilities of boundaries feeling of security of a good conscience of simplicity.

This is Holsinger's love, thus Styme Bow's revolving through the universe! Shinvescarine among presence and clear known pillar of cloud, pillar of fier, the Sun and the Moon came for a witness toward darkness heavens firmament. Black, but comely what things the excellency existent "zistense" upon hell living holds life alive and liveth keys visioning method, what knowledge accounting Venus retrograde earth 243 days Holsinger. I was born on a rock, stones time and developed space, reasons responds realistic funding spread self realization living death, breath of life with the body and yet whom which you from me of yet, you give I may be imaginative at self development treasure and practical life economic, creative impressing learning.

And Shinvescarine earth's dress, that moment time and thunder grow dark with lightning. Shall she'devil the attire of woman and subtil of hart, peace vows with harlots face and loud feet, good and living her help'meet, bone of bone and flesh naked, devilish girlish figurine of flesh. "[ARMAGEDDON]" psychiatrics transfer neurologics' neuron cells, atomic multiplicity askance of "protons means" pronouncing proof endemic physico allotment truncation tedious sedimentary epidermal lucent, third domestic growth precursor web, neuro'psycho motor system every online ethic "[Sand Tac Claus]" good wash medicinal Lab bus, Sea'Lab'Bus wrinkle elbow wind down management Vaso access plexi acting, Venus retrograde 243 earthlink days knowledgeable image on spectacle understanding Teth=Neth=Babb=Ye= Arms=Back=Thigh=Knese and legs, feet twinkling Gib'Ral'-Tar rock, keystone is roof, Faith Holsinger rock: My name is GIB'RAL'-TAR, I am this planet physical living STYME BOW World Holsinger Ministries Limited "[Shinvescarine of Heaven]".

Chapter 10
Destiny's Child

The image existing life arrangements, self discovery view, found preying heavy among value acknowledging the acceptable usages.

A man brings a beautiful message, if, I fall in love, because a need I have is fulfilled through creating a bond, then I love someone, really love them. What does this feeling generate in me? I think about the object of my love and affection! I think about them, I speak of them often and whenever possible I communicate with them and most of all want to be with them. I give them symbols of love, this inclination along with its rotation as we know here acting which, we learn to love the bond, that maturity assiduous bond the assiduity is love. Good things work for those to whom love is loving makeshifting the expertise as bouncing curves flexibility anew with tantamount firm reciprocity "enzyme'engines" form supple expertise accounting, love. This is the gist of love and the love for life I am alive, I need you like a shadow need a light, it was love that moved wanting to give life and living, there is even desire as I love, existence as I moved. Drawn loving, you will love upon the face of the deep, upon the face of the waters, love me and I am you, love me, love you. Yet, you see, which you see, self development learning, this is the love, that I will love that loveth me! The evidence of love and loyalty, we learn to love, to whom love, who wait for it. The "Key to Love", love thine neighbour as well as thine self. This approach is to what the "WORD of FAITH" is, don't be stupid being led by the sense of this WORLD. Resembling further living at the "MERCY" of the school of hard knocks, survivalists from the school of hard'knocks, of the justice system that states:

You can have Book knowledge, but, that doesn't mean You have an Education. Days length the understanding! Education means, You take responsibility. If, You take on responsibility, You take understanding! You take understanding, You take on responsibility! You have an Education. The doctrine of conscience of conscious state and the existence of being this doctrine of which I speak, therefore is beloved. Love is the active concern for the growth of that life which you exist. The body of the facts principles, accumulated by understanding the awareness, life is good, life is sweet with many and happy days, with many extraordinary graces, so you might be the wonder of this world forward felicity, whom and how much is being true reality and some thick palpable clouds of darkness.

Everything has its price, your life cost a heart'beat and your lungs the breath of life. Gum gleam, glime, go glip, glip, glip, glip, glip, glip Goo. "Mercy"! It is desire that you experience and love and love understood loves you to the life being, cause they acknowledge it, they hear and they understand Shinvescarine. You collect interest on what you put in the bank. The idiot and the wydiot, the wydiot stands for what'd he hit you with. The idiot is the Principal dunce of the Two-dummies, upgrading with a specific building of variables, that give to the determination of conservation technique of an utilization to determine! You collect interest on what you put in the bank. The central idiocy and to imagination, thereby lay conscious rise in the Air, things visibility, be the most humanitarian employing presence. I am in possession of my faculties, my accounts made of transacting states forming the specific reason for reference attached the amount, I have attempted to charge on my accounting the appropriate amount revolving credit. Now, at this moment, what you are really talking about, when you realize it, grinning stares window to the living, we all think that is to this realism [Heart'felt] attempt to articulate the question of Faith. While I thus act calling Voice upon this time of proof of the pudding that things senses visibility writing that word, imagines a word, so, loved life, love. Which you love, the reason I love, it is the breadth of life, used beloved. To be aware is to be alive and to be alive is to look, listen and live. The spirit and soul of man is the candle of searching rule over his flesh, Cup me, Laddle, Laddle, One Two, I make love and a Malt shook'up. Find life and find me as glory of clouds countenance is rain. Faith is the existence asking reason, responding faith to awash.

The Story of Beauty! It is considered to be of every naked thing brought meaning, we may eat of the fruit. What things counting flourishing performance accounting desire of my lips, "Cup-with-Handle" of my heart, it was love, If you love life and want that living, life explains love. You should get an understanding the particular desire of a certain choice and pleasure and purpose. I beg to defer from your thoughts as I am only a Man, which I be seated the World, Yet, I am bound, you will love and live according so, changes the "heart" that now, I love and life is love. That your hearts their true happiness maintaining the desire, which is because of the fruit thereof time spent to this world by hearing life and its meaning too live.

Every human beings form and content, life and its meaning to live, globe existence on a rock rolling stone and character with which you see it, life of members that by you and this thing whereas life of being thereof body and members, the existence of self, and the evidence of love and loyalty existence and feeling, so much so, as well as to give other needs and desires destiny's child. Sometimes to awake out of sleep leading to the darkness of the mind the thing that hath been, it is that which shall be and that which is done is that which shall be done and there is no new thing under the Sun, for I make a noise, because of the voice day and night they go upon it. Cup me, Laddle, Laddle, One' Two, understanding self esteem, courage self worth, love and specific self image is your responsibility to self expression needs and feelings, specific skills theme and blessing. Life is good to me, for I wonder. Life is good, life is sweet. That is how I continue to be treated. Life is good every day and this how I want to stay. That is why I sing this song for I praise Shinvescarine, every day long.

Beyonce Knowles can you handle it? Kelly Rowland can you handle it? Michelle Williams can you handle it? Destiny's Child You gotta Handle on it. Being that I am substance awareness, this approach to what is the WORD being Faith responding sense of WORLD reason seen thoughts. To ability, creativity and the average ideas, language imaginative aiming self'development, solving resolve of growth and change essence aim, whole issue approach, which the universal language is which describes knowledge along knowledge of character. Time and time again I have the satisfaction that I have everything, finally my "Aeroplanea" has come, arrived that change of seeing real-time at trying I well remember love, it is desire that you experience! Yet, the existing WORD as cloud countenance is rain. The existence understanding pleasant places. How much time have you invested improving improvement? What is it you have done, to the present time you know your job is living with what you think. The existence, the act and fact experience of all living methods, the passage of life instituting SHINVESCARINE access translating wilderness spread through Heaven's Cosmology brought TAR, realistic fund symbolism refunds doctrine aegis, it is truth first to give you to discover, of course the celebrated writing of act, running an exchange of imaginative glossary the central idiocy, superstition and imagination I, me, too realize to thereby lay conscience "aeroplanea" bacterium move aerobe sonic supersonic aesthete ethereal the upper atmosphere ooze and coil afferent pledging toward change a nerve of star, particular philosophy of beauty. Visibility employing majik rise "aeroplanea" visibility its revolving, be the most humanitarian employing pre'=sense, attractive existentialism that light, stars, flash lightning.

There is something "pathetic" about a [will=she=make=it=moment] when a girl stands steady with girly, giddy, gosh wonder and worship. When everyone's wondering just how she does it, like My somalian friend Rhoda Ahmed. She is "sexy" and she is given the [role] she plays, free of danger, the space of Femininity verging penetration the erotic fantasy with her captivated mind watching where she wants to go at any moment, feminine allure as a language of being [sexy] on a pedestal: we live each, day by day, each life. There are Rainy days and Sunny days! Nightfalls and Daylight and You Work and You Play and You Love.

You know the mentality a girl feels, when she puts the organ of sex inside of her mouth and plays the old skinflute: she ask, can I ask you something! Why, did you want me to put you in my mouth? Answer me, can you at least talk to me? OH MY GOD, it doesn't speak, it just spits.

I, pledge the allegiance toward that being "6" inches long for which it stands in the mouth in the name of "DAMON" we are together, feeding the fire, I, put you on a pedestal: I, put you on a pedestal it was better head. I, put you on a pedestal, your mouth is sweet and your head came upon me too rest. I, put you on a pedestal, butter'sweet as I left your lips. Your face beheld by my fingertips.

Human'beings sexualism mitigating conscience all thine heart, mind and body uncerstanding, just what works, you are giving to the body.

Just what works, you are giving to the body to the present time that you see acknowledging "center of thought" perceptibly a flame an flicker predacious fulfillment, we identify with being smarter reasons. Now, at this moment "pray'tell" thereupon realizing to understand what I mean, we all think that is toward this realism, to identify with convenience and toward the extenuating fullness brought to upon this time.

Destiny's Child, whose emphasis is on involvement, durability importantly of first truth, structure and memories that things are evidence alive one senses feeling well attended by existing that living life that you love, the expanse of these things I state realtime apparent honoure. You get the picture? Survival is of the fittest. For a species to survive, it has to acknowledge that there is the awareness of being conscious at some instigating method, this is with the accordance of selective annotating states. The inspiring divine inspirational law with life

issues suited to acknowledge order, relativity and forms cross polleniza-
tion. Relationships are built on compromise! When you're alone, You
can be as self indulgent as you want. But, when you're with another,
you have to adjust to them, this results revolving gist, being due of personal growth. Tell me, about being beautiful! Tell me, about tomorrow! Tell me, about love! Tell me, about curious countries ranges! To
extenuating time, identifying by understanding radicalism. To understand what we identify, upon this time. The extenuating fullness to
identify with convenience and to understand what I mean to acknowledge awareness, some instigating method selective accordance of being
honoure apparent, suited to acknowledge annotating convergence at
some instigating relativity and forms, sharing, I do for you and you do
for me and we do for each other, together. Personalism you can wear,
jewelry you can wear, pocketbooks you can carry, maps you draw,
pouches retrieve a story you write! Starting the access relay, availability
awaits the ability to get, Vice and Versa and simply with world views,
everywhere you want to be, its your life, explicit where you live and
what you want. We've all got plenty to learn, some form of experience
for, both pleasure orgasms and desires, We live as a world with pleasure
to talk about sex, sometimes to the main act, pure of course even
though real life and behavioures depicted, pleasure is a truth tempting.
I can say this for sure! Home is much smoother, being home "Moon-
walking" nativity whispery intensity of sex appeal, what's Luv'? All the
things that we accept. The backbone appeal self assured, remains to us
that which reminds the affirmativeness of spirit. Who emotions
grunt'work, glimpses most luminous moment churning respect giving
what matters though riding experimenting ability superfluous raw real-
time in the making, just a matter of applying more elbow grease.

This "Year" marks a milestone at its best, promoting satisfaction rec-
onciling the needs we consume most viable. Shaped by an understanding that addresses human legacy with, state of the art finesse and why
you should be there "Jingle Bill". Erotic melodrama and some serious
soul searching. Be a fast thinker to create emotionally rich the spirit

with its move as good as it gets. This Years celebrating spirit and the love around the globe adopts both live underlining sustainable ideal relations which will star development, and to acquire among them the optimism seen as it created a Hothouse atmosphere. Je 'ne-' se'-quoi meaning, I don't know what?

C'est la vie and that's just the way it is.

Independent Bishop, Damon Ray Hollingsworth PH.D.

A Short Biography about the Author*

Damon Ray Hollingsworth PH.D. was born May 28th 1952, Time: 6:12AM BlackPlanet, Gemini as Styme Bow World, Camelist, Came-lus; Camelism'Camel live image of man. Travels global living the entertainment style of Stage Acting/Writing/Singing. Born the United States Indian, Caucasian African American BrownSkin, My friends call me Gib'Ral'-Tar.

0-595-23432-1

www.ingramcontent.com/pod-product-compliance
Lightning Source LLC
Chambersburg PA
CBHW020257290526
45784CB00003B/1284